THE

CHARLESTON

ACADEMY

OF

DOMESTIC

PURSUITS

THE

CHARLESTON ACADEMY

OF

DOMESTIC PURSUITS

A HANDBOOK OF ETIQUETTE WITH RECIPES

SUZANNE POLLAK & LEE MANIGAULT

ILLUSTRATIONS BY TANIA LEE

STEWART, TABORI & CHANG
NEW YORK

Published in 2014 by
Stewart, Tabori & Chang
An imprint of Abrams

Library of Congress Control Number: 2013945636

ISBN: 978-1-61769-086-0

Designer: Deb Wood
Production manager: Anet Sirna-Bruder

Printed and bound in China
10 9 8 7 6 5 4 3 2 1

Stewart, Tabori & Chang books are available at special discounts
when purchased in quantity for premiums and promotions as well as
fundraising or educational use. Special editions can also be created
to specification. For details, contact specialsales@abramsbooks.com
or the address below.

ABRAMS
THE ART OF BOOKS SINCE 1949
115 WEST 18TH STREET
NEW YORK, NY 10011
WWW.ABRAMSBOOKS.COM

TO THE GODFATHER

OF THIS BOOK,

WILLIAM LEA THOMPSON

PART III: MASTER CLASS 147

PART IV: THE DEANS CONCLUDE 203

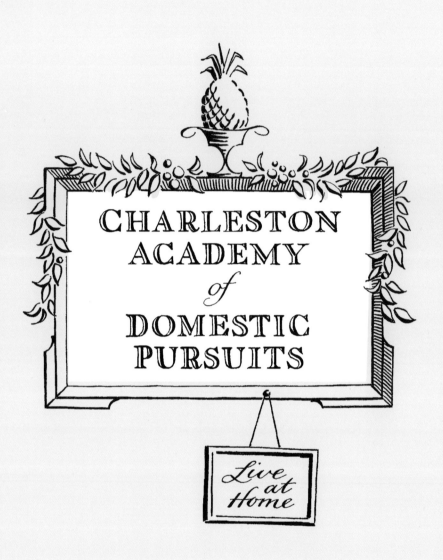

CHARLESTON
ACADEMY
of
DOMESTIC
PURSUITS

Live at Home

NESTLED DEEP IN THE SOUTH is a tiny academy that teaches the most important classes in the world: our Academy of Domestic Pursuits. Students want to go to Harvard for academics, but when they need to know how to live at home, they send their applications to us.

Why? Because we hold the only PhDs in "Food and Its Many Uses" and "Managing a Household" ever awarded. To become the two most knowledgeable authorities in our respective fields, we each spent decades running our houses and logged thousands of miles spanning all the continents poking our noses into other cultures, all while raising six children between us. The stunningly good news for you is that we are overly generous, and we've distilled down and culled out the most important information so that you do not have to spend the majority of *your* life figuring out the best ways to live at home. This handbook is our gift to you.

We are Suzanne Pollak and Lee Manigault and we have been living for years in the most genteel city in the entire country. We founded the Charleston Academy of Domestic Pursuits because if *we* don't show you where to place your silver iced tea spoon on the table, who will? We know not only precisely where to seat everyone for a dinner party, but also exactly who stands where for cocktails. And we want you to understand that it *is* possible to remove a drunken reveler with grace and humor without clearing out the rest of your guests. We know all these secrets, and many more. We are, after all, the Deans of the Academy.

One day, Lee spied the ever-chic Suzanne across a crowded room and knew at once they would be fast friends. Immediately, Lee invited Suzanne to a dinner party at her house. Lee answered the door in a long evening dress and bare feet, her favorite go-to attire for at-home entertaining. Not surprisingly, it is also Suzanne's. In fact, everything about the evening reminded Suzanne of the way she likes to entertain. Could Lee be her long-lost soul mate? Just maybe. . . .

They went for coffee the next day, and before the first latte was finished, The Charleston Academy of Domestic Pursuits had been born. Dean Manigault found herself finishing Dean Pollak's sentences, and vice versa. Each Dean thought she knew all there was to know about gracious living, but upon finding her domestic twin, the Deans realized that there was an endless amount left to learn. Like Aristotle and Plato before them, the Deans debated for hours on end. Their pursuit of domesticity was the same, but there were crucial differences. Dean Manigault was astounded to hear that Dean Pollak insists on a wet brine for her chicken while Dean Manigault had been dry brining for years. Dean Pollak was floored when she discovered that Dean Manigault wouldn't consider drinking wine out of a stemless glass, because Dean Pollak had gone stemless at her first opportunity.

Once the union had been formed, the inevitability of the pairing was obvious to all. For, though leisurely entertainments were wildly abundant twenty years ago, it dawned on us that we were among the last two people still dragging out our dining tables under the live oak trees for candlelight suppers. If even people *here*, in this last bastion of civility, were not taking the trouble to live graciously, we shuddered to think what must be happening nationwide. We have munificently taken upon our shoulders the burden of relighting the way for all.

We realized soon after opening the Academy that, tragically, not everyone can attend our seminars in person, no matter how great their need. A textbook was mandatory so that our lessons could reach everyone. Enrobed in our Dean's gowns, we sat down to put to paper our mighty message—and the book wrote itself. After reading only a few pages, each reader will realize that the most crucial truths of pleasurable living are held within these pages. Happily, as essential as these truths are, learning them is well within everyone's grasp.

We are two experts who are not afraid to tell you what to do. We have been living in, and proudly running, our houses for twenty-five years. People ask our advice all the time because they can see that we enjoy living in our houses — and we make it look easy. This is because we have put so much thought and energy into how we do our jobs around the house. We celebrate everything. One of us gave an Emancipation Proclamation dinner dance on a moonlit barrier island when she got divorced, while the other hosted a Go Green dinner when her son mowed the lawn without being asked.

The Academy's main lecture hall is the kitchen, because in our houses, as well as yours, this room is the beating heart of the house. Every person, every day, asks this key life question: "What's for dinner?" The Charleston Academy of Domestic Pursuits Handbook answers the question in multiple ways. We are dismayed that so many people use their kitchens only as a place to store mail and to throw away takeout boxes. This book is a defibrillator for kitchens everywhere.

Let the Deans give you the best recipes for avoiding boredom. When your kitchen entices with good food and aromas, your family gathers, and a sense of calm and conviviality quickly follows. Soon, your family wants to share this fun with other people, and they bring their friends by to enjoy a meal. In no time your house is the place where people congregate to enjoy themselves. Voilà! You have become a competent host.

The Deans recoil when we hear that people are intimidated by cooking. We have taken it upon ourselves to eliminate any kitchen roadblocks—and we hold your hand to help you overcome your fears. Our first course covers every-thing from brining to blanching—plus every other kitchen skill you might need.

Once we have covered kitchen basics, we move right on to what's in season. Here in the Low Country we know that the four seasons are actually deer, dove, duck, and turkey. At the Academy, we will teach you how to roast a pig in your backyard, as well as how to preserve excess bounty from the garden. We suspect that Lilly Pulitzer must have had a conference with Mother Nature to design the bright-colored watermelon, which we love to pickle, and we salivate just thinking about the exotic chutneys from Rajasthan—not surprisingly, our Jam and Pickling classes are the first to sell out each spring. We transfer each class's enthusiasm right to the pages of this book, so that people as far away as Istanbul can feel like they've spent a weekend with us at the Academy.

Of course, we cannot be on call for our students twenty-four hours a day. We need time to unwind. Let us reteach you the custom of taking a half-hour cocktail break. In the Academy laboratory, we've created salubrious and restorative cocktails using rum, bourbon, vodka, tequila, and Champagne (just not all in the same drink, mind you).

Once you're refreshed, you can turn to the chapter on training staff— the ones you gave birth to, the ones you have hired, and the majordomo you married. A few chores done by all every night enhance communal living, not only for children but for spouses as well. After your staff has been fully brought up to speed, entertaining will be a snap.

Now you are ready to entertain. Take houseguests, for instance. We educate the guest and host alike, and in the Academy lab we've perfected formulas for everything from the correct length of stay to the perfect hostess gifts. We assert that the best part of having houseguests is the opportunity to cook a lavish breakfast. Some of the most fun we have ever had is cooking and eating breakfast with our overnight guests (even our relatives).

Etiquette is a topic with which people seem to have a love-hate relationship. People like to think that etiquette is not relevant, but the lightest scratching of the surface reveals that just about every student actually pines to know which fork to use, how long a cocktail hour should be, where to seat the loser husband of an old friend, and myriad other arcana. We have found that a solid grounding in manners frees people to find their comfort zone. If you know why or how things are supposed to be done, then you will feel more comfortable changing or ignoring what does not suit you. In this book we have compiled the questions and answers from our past classes. Our instructions will help ease the mind of polite, eager students everywhere.

Gracious living is for everyone. We hear the collective sigh of relief as readers realize how little extra effort is required to incorporate the Charleston Academy's ethos into everyday life. We can visualize thousands of friends and families relaxing and enjoying each other's company. Living life as an Academy grad will make your life twice as charming.

RULE #1
HOME

A WELL-RUN HOUSE IS THE
BEDROCK TO A SUCCESSFUL
LIFE FOR EACH INHABITANT.

RULE #2
HEART

USING YOUR KITCHEN TO CREATE
HOME-COOKED MEALS WILL RESULT
IN A HEALTHIER AND HAPPIER LIFE.

RULE #3
HOSPITALITY

ENTERTAINING AT HOME IMPROVES
YOUR LIFE IN WAYS THAT YOU
CANNOT EVEN IMAGINE.

PART 1

ELEMENTARY EDUCATION

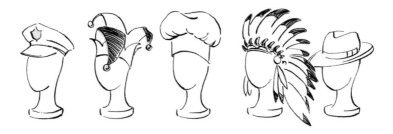

"The kitchen wears many hats."

ORGANIZATION:

The Kitchen Wears Many Hats

At one time or another the Deans' kitchens have served as dining rooms, offices, playrooms, homework stations, living rooms, wineries, and even penal colonies. A room this integral to family life has to be organized for maximum efficiency or the owner can't exploit all its advantages.

Kitchens require a multitude of ambiances. A dimmer switch for overhead lighting is necessary for all the activities the kitchen will host. There is no way to do homework without plenty of lighting; conversely, there is no way to relax with your glass of wine under klieg lights.

Kitchens crave order. The kitchen should be a *transitory* area for coats, backpacks, mail, and pocketbooks—not their final resting place. Every afternoon Dean Manigault's daughters do their homework and science experiments in the kitchen. To start cooking the nightly dinner, Dean Manigault needs a leaf blower and bullhorn to have extra paper and books removed from the countertop. After your meal, keep in mind that dirty dishes do not improve with age, so get in there and get them clean. Keeping your kitchen tidy is a good habit to form early and practice often.

If possible, kitchen gadgets should be put away when not in use. Finding out-of-sight homes for the food processor, blender, etc., is the quickest way to declutter your kitchen. However, the coffee maker is used every day, so this creator of lifeblood has earned its counter space, and the standing mixer is so heavy that you'll never want to move it.

If you have a bad back, like Dean Pollak, where you place your heavy pots is important. A hanging rack is essential for her physical well-being and not merely a decorative element. Unless you are as tall as LeBron James, teetering on top of stools and countertops to retrieve items from way up high is dangerous and unsustainable. Cupboard shelves that extend all the way to the ceiling are only appropriate for storage items that are rarely used. Once something has been put this far out of sight, you will forget its very existence.

ELEMENTARY EDUCATION　　17

Even the Deans need motivation to get our kitchens in order. Sometimes, it's not until we're inviting six to ten of our well-heeled friends over for a gathering that we look at our kitchens through their eyes and say, "Oh, boy! We've got some work to do." The Deans roll up our sleeves and tackle one area at a time, working our way around the room. Do not let yourself get so carried away that you store anything in the oven. Believe it or not, the Deans have actually seen this done! We start tidying several days before our jump-up, not twenty minutes before guests walk in. Now our party has served two purposes: to reconnect with friends and to return the kitchen to a state of Zen. Be sure to clean up after guests leave, also, or all the hard work will have been in vain.

When the Deans are shopping for food for a specific recipe, we put all the ingredients for this recipe in one bag. Then we refrigerate the bag in its entirety—that way, we don't have to hunt and peck for ingredients or forget any. The ancillary items we already own, we get out before we start cooking. If you do this, you won't mess with your timetable by having to do a last-minute search. This is part of *mise en place*, a fancy culinary way of saying, "Get your ducks in a row," or preparing all your ingredients, equipment, and utensils so they're at hand when you begin to cook. Each chopped item, liquid, or dry good gets premeasured and put in its separate bowl. Get in the habit of the proper *mise en place*! The Deans' mantra is "Don't sleaze your mise." Cooking cannot be fun or relaxing when fear of catastrophe looms overhead, so it's no wonder people can drink a whole bottle of wine while cooking their nightly meal if they never got in the habit of a proper mise.

Just as important as *mise en place* is cleaning utensils, countertops, and dishes as you proceed with your recipes. Any moment that you're not sautéing or mixing and your eyes and hands can be diverted should be spent washing up. By the end of cooking, you won't be faced with a disastrous mess—you'll have a clean kitchen *and* a delicious meal.

Leftovers need to be monitored. Nothing repulses the Deans more than spying long-forgotten items in the back or bottom of the refrigerator. Rotten food casts a shadow of doubt on the freshness of all the contents of your fridge. Rotate leftovers to the front of the shelves so you don't lose sight of what you have.

Similarly, a pantry in chaos is useless. If the cans, boxes, and jars are out of date, then your pantry is a graveyard. Not only is your money being wasted, so is your time, because you'll have to run out at the last minute and purchase items that should be at your fingertips. Be sure to keep an eye on expiration dates. Dried herbs and spices are especially vulnerable. Just like Baby New Year turns into decrepit Father Time, so, too, do these seasonings disintegrate into dung-colored dust. You're fooling yourself, but no one else, if you think you're adding flavor to your food with these outdated additives. The Deans insist you assiduously check your cabinets and keep your spices for no more than a year. When in doubt, throw it out.

MUST-HAVES:

School Supplies

COOKBOOKS We can't emphasize strongly enough the importance of jotting your ideas in the margins of your cookbooks. First and foremost, note whether you even like the recipe. It may seem impossible to believe, but after years of cooking you will forget what you have cooked, let alone whether the recipe was tasty or not. Next, write down any tweaks you made or wish to make next time. Was the heat high enough? Would you add more cumin? Would you double the quantities? You can even remark on who ate the meal with you and what they thought of it, if relevant. We are not advocating writing an entire new cookbook in the margin, but you and your future grandchildren will treasure your pithy comments later on.

The Deans have collected thousands of cookbooks over the decades and the walls of our kitchens are libraries. We still get misty-eyed about the ones we gave away, when we deluded ourselves in the thought that we had too many. The older the book, the better, because not long ago very few chefs took the time to write a book, and those who did had groundbreaking recipes in their minds and on their stoves. Having purchased our book, you're well on your way to a stellar cookbook collection.

KITCHENAID OR OTHER STANDING MIXER This is a large, heavy piece of equipment and has an expensive price tag. However, the initial outlay pays off. Both Deans have had ours for more than two decades and we use them at least once a week. If you amortize the price over twenty years, the mixer is probably the cheapest thing in the kitchen. Dean Manigault's KitchenAid has outlasted her marriage by at least a decade. The Deans wish that every relationship we had was as constant and reliable as the one we have had with our respective standing mixers.

SILPAT, ROUL'PAT, OR OTHER SILICONE BAKING SHEET

Even your emotionally neediest family member cannot help but feel loved when presented with a slice of homemade pie. A silicone baking sheet is what makes that pie possible, because it's essential for rolling out flaky dough. Gone are the days of scraping your countertop to remove sticky dough remnants. Now you just roll out your dough on the silicone. Biscuits and silicone are a marriage that no man should tear asunder. After being folded and refolded, the biscuits will rise to towering heights. Cookies can be baked on the silicone. How one piece of rubber can be all things to all doughs, we'll never know.

THE ACADEMY'S SOUTHERN BISCUIT

We don't care who you are—nobody has the time or desire to make a flaky croissant first thing in the morning. If you are making croissants, then you are baking four hundred of them and opening up a patisserie. We assert that pastry has personality; the croissant is haughty and refined. The biscuit, on the other hand, is a plucky little fireplug with a can-do attitude. He is the friend to every meal and will even do appetizer duty if you but ask. He has a wide-open smile ready to accommodate ham or melted butter. He just wants to be loved. Folding the pastry a few times creates layers—a nod to its French cousin, the croissant. *MAKES 12 TO 18, depending on size of biscuit cutter*

3 cups self-rising flour,
    preferably White Lily
1 tablespoon baking powder
1 teaspoon salt
½ teaspoon baking soda
1 stick (4 ounces) unsalted
    butter, cut into 4 equal pieces
1½ cups whole buttermilk

Preheat the oven to 500°F.

In a large bowl, whisk together the flour, baking powder, salt, and baking soda. Using two knives or a pastry blender, cut the butter into the flour until it forms pea-size pieces.

Add the buttermilk and stir with a wooden spoon until the dough almost forms a ball.

Place the dough on a silicone baking mat and begin folding up the sides, right and left, until a ball forms. Using a rolling pin, roll out the dough to ½-inch thickness. Fold one side of the dough into the center and then fold in the other side. Roll out again and refold in the same manner three to six times. (Each roll and fold creates flaky layers within your biscuits.) Roll out one final time until the dough is ¾ inch thick.

Cut out biscuits with a 2-inch biscuit cutter or an inverted glass.

Place the biscuits on a nonstick baking sheet. Gather the scraps, reroll, and cut out more biscuits until all of the dough has been used. (At this point, you can cover the unbaked biscuits with plastic wrap and refrigerate for up to 24 hours, or freeze for up to 3 weeks.)

Bake until lightly browned on the top and bottom, 10 to 12 minutes. (Bake frozen biscuits at 425°F for 25 minutes.)

SKILLET The Deans are in complete agreement that the skillet is the most-used item in both our kitchens. We disagree on which ones we prefer. We both own cast-iron, nonstick, and sticky skillets. Each pan has its own uses. Dean Manigault finds herself reaching for her cast iron for almost every meal, whereas Dean Pollak is forever yoked to her 9-inch nonstick. Our skillet cupboard puts our shoe racks to shame.

SAUTÉED CARROTS AND PEACHES

SERVES 4 TO 6

1 tablespoon olive oil
1 bunch carrots with
    tops, washed and peeled
Coarse salt, for sprinkling
Ground cumin, for sprinkling
1 peach, peeled and sliced
Freshly ground black pepper

Heat the oil in a large skillet over medium heat. Add the carrots and toss to coat in the oil. Season with salt and cumin. Cook until the carrots are browned on the outside, about 10 to 20 minutes.

During the last 5 minutes, add the peach slices and toss with the carrots. Season with pepper.

CRUNCHY SHALLOTS

With the possible exception of ice cream (and we can't be sure because we haven't tried it) there is not one dish that a scattering of crunchy shallots does not improve. Everyone will think you are a cooking genius if you simply fry one thinly sliced shallot per person and sprinkle the shatteringly crisp shards over the meal. Be sure to drain on a paper towel to remove excess oil.

1 shallot per person, sliced as thinly as possible

Olive oil, for frying

In a small saucepan, pour enough olive oil to reach a depth of ½ inch. Heat over high heat. Add a few sliced shallots to test the temperature, adjusting the heat so the shallots turn golden brown, not instantly black, which will happen if your oil is too hot.

Remove the shallots with a slotted spoon and transfer to paper towels to drain while cooking the remaining slices. The shallots will stay crisp for up to an hour or two.

BLENDER Dean Manigualt hides cruciferous vegetables in her various smoothies for added health benefits in her children's breakfast. In the evening, the Deans hide extra rum in our daiquiris for added mental health benefits. Most days it's hard to tell which one is more salubrious.

For those of you who prefer your juicer to your blender, we are big enough to admit we are jealous of your fulltime staff. The juicer requires a dedicated personal attendant to keep it clean. Additionally, your drink is not as healthy as you think. Juicers remove all the fiber from fruits and vegetables, so your beverage raises your glycemic index because there is no fiber to counterbalance the sugar during digestion.

teakettle   wooden spoons   mortar & pestle

SMOOTHIE

On a yoga retreat at OmBase Yoga, the Zen master presented us with this smoothie, and we were smitten. We know you will be, too. It's appropriate for all diets, except someone with a nut allergy. The measurements are not exact because some people like a thick yogurtlike consistency that requires a spoon, while others prefer a liquid that's sippable right out of a glass. The choice is yours. If you use frozen fruit, use less ice. Namaste. *SERVES 2*

1 cup strawberries or other berries, frozen

1 cup ice cubes

1 cup water

½ cup raw almonds, cashews, or walnuts (preferably soaked for several hours in water)

½ medium avocado

1 tablespoon chia seeds, soaked for at least 30 minutes and up to overnight

2 to 3 tablespoons pure maple syrup

1 to 2 teaspoons pure vanilla extract

2 to 3 drops Wild Orange essential oil, preferably doTerra or other ingestible brand (optional)

Puree all the ingredients together in a sturdy blender. We can already see your inner glow.

CITRUS JUICER/EXTRACTOR   Fresh-squeezed orange juice and popovers are a tough breakfast to beat. Dean-in-training Gigi Manigault passes along her top juicing tips: 1) Get your mom to shell out for the one-armed Breville juicer. This machine puts all other juicers to shame. Gigi goes through a bag of oranges in five minutes flat—it takes longer for her to cut them than to juice them. 2) Crucial: Clean your juicer immediately after use because wet pulp can be wiped away with ease, but dry pulp is intractable. 3) Juicing is a job that must be done at the last minute. Fresh citrus juice waits for no man.

MICROWAVE The Deans wildly disagree about the microwave. Dean Manigault can't live without hers and Dean Pollak won't live *with* one. Dean Pollak's children are so confounded by her aversion that on two separate occasions they have gifted her one, which she promptly regifted right back to them. Clutter on her countertops drives her far crazier than reheating coffee on the stove or putting stews and casseroles back into the oven for a gentle reheat. She has never trusted what's going on inside that box and refuses to eat anything that comes out of it.

TEAKETTLE The Deans think that a beautiful teakettle is an investment piece. A gleaming copper teakettle whistling away on the stovetop is even better than a man whistling at you: A man comes with all his inherent problems but a teakettle promises only a calming cup of tea that can't but help improve any situation. If cups of tea could sooth the jangled nerves of Londoners under German bombardment during World War II, surely a cup of tea can help you get through whatever your day has wrought. The teakettle is the only item that lives on the stovetop and therefore its appearance is part of your kitchen's décor.

WOODEN SPOON A wooden spoon must be one of the oldest tools in the kitchen. The minute our ancestors started cooking over flames, they needed something to stir with and so created the wooden spoon. The Deans' wooden spoons have been scorched, boiled, cracked, and overwashed, but we love them above all other tools in our kitchens.

TONGS Between the Deans we own twelve pairs of tongs. Professional chefs taught us that piercing cooking meats with a fork to turn or test them while cooking creates a tunnel out of which pour all the juices and flavor you have worked so hard to create. Grabbing the meat with a pair of tongs to flip eliminates this problem. The skillet's right-hand man is his tongs.

FRIED ONION RINGS

Fried onion rings are delicious. We've never met anyone, including ourselves, who could eat just one. They are a perfect hors d'oeuvres when you are having people over for a drink, and a welcome snack for your kids to munch on when they are doing their homework. The Deans prefer fried onions to fried potatoes and we serve them on hamburger night, steak night, and dinner-party night. Caveat: Fried onion rings need to be eaten as soon as they crisp up. The minute they are cool enough to touch, they are stale.

At this very point in the book, we'd like to honor Caroline Trask, who so thoroughly incorporates gracious living into her life that she doesn't even know there is another way. The Deans did not spring out of the ocean fully formed—we learned at the knees of some of the country's most esteemed and practiced doyennes and hostesses. Whether Caroline is entertaining in the city, at her beach house, or on her plantation, her guests never worry for an instant that the excitement they are about to experience will be anything less than perfection. From the first tinkle of her silver bell, they know that they're in the presence a true master of Southern gentility. It was Caroline who put the fried onion ring trick up our sleeves: Make them months ahead and pull them out of the freezer when your guests arrive. Unbelievably, they are even better than the ones you would have made à la minute, not to mention your dress won't be stained with grease! Also unbelievably, after twenty years of constant begging by the Deans, Caroline has finally been worn down and shared her recipe with us. We couldn't stand to make you wait twenty years, so here it is. *SERVES 6 TO 8*

One 12-ounce can beer (1½ cups), at room temperature
1½ cups unbleached all-purpose flour
1 teaspoon salt

Vegetable oil or vegetable shortening, for frying
2 to 3 onions, thinly sliced crosswise into rings

In a bowl, whisk together the beer, flour, and salt. Let rest at room temperature, stirring occasionally, for at least 3 hours.

In a large, deep skillet, add enough oil to reach a depth of 2 inches. Heat until a deep-fat thermometer registers 375°F. Dip the onion rings in the beer batter to coat. Using tongs, transfer the rings, in batches, to the hot oil and fry until golden (watch carefully to avoid burning).

Transfer the fried rings to paper-towel- or brown-paper-bag-lined baking sheets to drain. (Mrs. Trask suggests covering each layer with wax paper and then covering the whole package in foil before freezing. She says they freeze beautifully for as long as three months.)

When ready to serve, preheat the oven to 400°F. Place the rings in a single layer on a baking sheet and bake until hot, 5 to 10 minutes at the most.

MORTAR AND PESTLE Dean Pollak cannot figure out why Dean Manigault has not replaced her lost mortar and pestle. What other kitchen tool has been around for thousands of years? The mortar and pestle is a talisman of the sophisticated cook. It extracts more flavors when grinding spices or creating pastes than a food processor, which chops but doesn't necessarily emulsify ingredients. The mortar and pestle is perfect for making pestos and grinding toasted whole spices.

FOOD PROCESSOR If you want a well-outfitted kitchen, you need a food processor. Our favorite is made by Cuisinart. When the Cuisinart first came on the scene, they were the IT item for the kitchen for twenty years. Entire cookbooks and magazines were devoted to this kitchen magician. Our blades may no longer be rotating a full twenty-four hours a day, but they rotate enough to warrant the food processor's inclusion in kitchen essentials. Dean Manigault uses her machine for making *gougères* and salsa verde, mincing lamb for shepherd's pie, and pureeing some soups. Dean Pollak uses the mini version to create mayonnaise, salad dressing, and gremolata.

MAYONNAISE

When you run out of Hellman's mayonnaise, whipping up a homemade version is faster than running to the store. This recipe takes five minutes to make! (Use a mini machine for making salad dressings and mayonnaise because the sauce gets stuck under the blades or on the sides of the large machine.) *MAKES 1½ CUPS*

2 large egg yolks, at room temperature
4 teaspoons fresh lemon juice
2 teaspoons Dijon mustard
2 teaspoons cold water
½ teaspoon coarse salt
1½ cups neutral vegetable oil, such as safflower or canola

Using a mini food processor, whip together the egg yolks, lemon juice, mustard, water, and salt. Insert the pusher into the feed tube of your food processor. There is a small hole in the pusher designed just to allow oil to drizzle during mayonnaise making. Fill pusher with oil. Repeat as necessary until all the oil is incorporated and the mayonnaise is thick, about 2 minutes. Store in the refrigerator for up to 6 days.

GREMOLATA

1 lemon
⅓ cup fresh parsley
3 cloves garlic

Remove the peel from the lemon using a vegetable peeler. Place peels, parsley, and garlic in a food processor and blend until well mixed, about 1 minute. Can be refrigerated for up to 6 hours before serving.

ACADEMY SALAD DRESSING

In making salad dressing, we noticed a little hot water aids the emulsification. Jean-Georges Vongerichten and Mark Bittman's book *Simple to Spectacular* recommends the same thing. Great minds think alike. *MAKES 1 CUP*

½ cup fresh lemon juice
½ cup olive oil

Salt and freshly ground black pepper
2 tablespoons hot water

Using a mini food processor, blend the lemon juice and olive oil; season with salt and pepper. Add the water and blend for 30 seconds.

The dressing will be creamy and perfect for all Academy salads. Store in the refrigerator for up to 3 days.

CUTTING BOARD If you have to ask us why you need one, then you have never stepped in your kitchen or anyone else's. This book is not for you.

STEEL KNIFE There is no serviceable kitchen that does not contain at least one high-quality knife. Don't be seduced by the mid-priced, "permanently sharp" variety—they are no good. Dean Manigault had a boyfriend who gave her a set of top-quality knives. She used them to cut his heart out, and she kept the knives. They improved the quality of her kitchen life immeasurably.

WOODEN BOWL The origins of the Academy lie in our wooden bowls. At least four out of five days a week the Academy lunchroom serves our famous salad in our wooden bowl. Since the salad changes daily, depending on the Deans' new favorite food fad, there is no opportunity for the bowl to get bored. Each day the bowl excitedly offers itself up to receive whatever masterpiece the Deans have created for lunch.

ALL-YEAR-LONG ACADEMY SALADS

Most people's salads are lettuce-centric and many of the Deans' favorites are, too, but *all* of our salads are crouton-based. An edifice built on a solid foundation will never crumble; similarly, a salad based on a hot fried crouton will never grow old.

The Deans jump in the Dean-mobile and head to the produce aisle of our local market. Upon entering the emporium our eyes start scanning for what is freshest and best and local. Sometimes a South American avocado will sneak its way into our cart, but in general we don't buy strawberries in December or butternut squash in August. What's available and freshest dictates what kind of salad we will be serving that day. We eschew writing specific salad recipes because we have never made the same one twice, so we can't expect you to. Picking tasty, ripe produce and mixing things together is the way to go. Raspberries can be mixed with beets; endive with pears and parsley; fennel with pomegranate seeds and orange wedges. We are giving you a few outlines, but you need to color the canvas yourself.

WINTER SALAD	SPRING SALAD	SUMMER SALAD	FALL SALAD
Roasted vegetables tossed with blue cheese, walnuts, and medium-size fried croutons	Endive, cucumber, fennel, and scallions macerated in lemon and salt, with small fried croutons	Plucked-from-the-garden tomatoes, buffalo mozzarella, basil, and extra-large round fried croutons to absorb the tomato juices	Pears, avocado, goat cheese, butter lettuce, and fried croutons (by now you are accomplished enough to choose your own crouton size)
PROTEIN OPTION: *sliced steak, hot or cold*	PROTEIN OPTION: *hot or cold crispy salmon*	PROTEIN OPTION: *thick-cut applewood-smoked bacon*	PROTEIN OPTION: *baked slices of prosciutto*

TWELVE-MONTHS-A-YEAR PARSLEY SALAD

Poor Little Parsley. As you steer your grocery cart into the produce section, those little green leaves whisper, "Don't forget me, I am just as tasty as the butter lettuce and romaine on the next shelf. In fact, I have a little kick that will wake up your taste buds. But somehow my leaves receive short shrift and are dismissed. I am not just a garnish!" The Deans decree the time has come for a parsley celebration.

The Deans are fans of both curly and flat-leaf parsley alike. Just be careful you don't pick cilantro, as it looks like flat-leaf parsley but tastes quite different. Be sure to smell the greens or read the label carefully to check. In this salad, flat-leaf parsley is the star—a bit of a departure from the usual lettuces. It's refreshing and we hear it is good for our breath. Healthful and beneficial. Cannot do better than that. *SERVES 4*

1 bunch scallions, thinly sliced
Juice of 1 lemon
Generous pinch of sea salt
1 persimmon, mango, or apple, peeled, cored, and diced
1 avocado, peeled, pitted, and diced into cubes

1 small piece salami, diced
2 bunches fresh flat-leaf or curly parsley, chopped
2 ounces blue cheese, crumbled

In a medium bowl, macerate the scallions with the lemon juice and salt while arranging the rest of your salad. Add your choice of seasonal fruit. Add the avocado (so loaded with health benefits that we believe everyone should eat 1 avocado every day!). Next, in goes the salami (it might seem like an odd salad addition but it really gives this salad its kick) and parsley. Top with the cheese.

* NOTE: *Don't grab the first blue cheese you see. Some are more than $30 per pound, others that will be just as delicious in this salad can be as little as $4.99. We always advocate using the best ingredients, but in this instance we have noticed that the price difference is just that—a price difference, not a quality or flavor difference.*

ACADEMY CROUTONS

The keystone of the Academy is our crouton. A warm, crunchy exterior yields to a delicate center, with a perfect oil-to-bread ratio. Olive oil is what makes the croutons delicious, even when you only have access to mediocre bread. The building blocks for a crouton include a skillet filled with the correct depth of oil (¼ inch), the proper size of bread (1 inch square), and patience (all sides of the crouton cube must be tended to). Using tongs, turn your croutons once one side is golden brown, being sure to minister to every exposed surface. A cold crouton is a useless crouton; so know that you will be making these at the last possible moment. *MAKES ENOUGH CROUTONS FOR 6 TO 8 SALADS*

1 loaf country-style bread,
    preferably sourdough
Olive oil, for frying

1 clove garlic, halved
    (optional)

Using a bread knife, cut the bread into 1-inch-thick slices (thick slices are the key to a tasty crouton). Cut off the crusts and cut the slices into ¾- to 1-inch cubes.

In a medium, nonstick skillet over medium heat, heat enough olive oil to come ¼ inch up the sides of the croutons. Slip the bread cubes into the pan in one layer. After a couple of minutes, when the bottom side is golden brown, turn the cubes to an uncooked side using tongs. You may want to lower the heat to medium-low if the croutons are getting too dark. Turn the cubes at least one more time. If you have made large croutons, you may rub the cut garlic clove on the surface of the croutons while they're warm.

Croutons can be served directly from the pan or at room temperature. They should be eaten within a half hour.

ROASTING PAN   A good roasting pan is expensive. You will never regret the money spent, but you will have to spend it. For your initial pan, go ahead and buy the Rolls-Royce. A best-quality roasting pan will last for generations and will be the ideal weight, size, and have the proper handles. The heaviness of the pan material means the heat disseminates evenly and discourages burning. The largest roasting pan that your oven can accommodate is the size you should purchase. Measure one of the racks of your oven and make sure your roasting pan is two inches smaller so the heat can circulate all around it.

ROASTED WINTER VEGETABLES

Go down the grocery store aisle and choose the tubers and gourds that appeal to you: beets, turnips, rutabaga, butternut squash, acorn squash, pumpkin. None of these are edible raw, but toss them in a little olive oil, put them in the oven for 45 minutes to an hour, and voilà! You now have the basis for side dishes, salads, soups, or a main course. These vegetables take initial peeling and chopping prep, but after that they are as versatile as the tender bounty of spring and just as colorful. We can't be too specific with this recipe because we don't know what is in your supermarket and what you like to eat. The principle for all winter root vegetables is the same. *SERVES 6 TO 8*

1 butternut squash, turnip,
    large parsnip, or rutabaga,
    peeled, seeded*, and cut
    into 1½-inch pieces

2 tablespoons olive oil
Salt and freshly ground black
    pepper

Preheat the oven to 375°F. Rub the cut vegetables with the olive oil and place on a baking sheet; season with salt and pepper. Roast until a knife tip inserts easily and the vegetable edges are slightly caramelized, about 45 minutes to 1 hour.

Do not throw away the squash seeds. They are wonderful washed, dried, lightly oiled, salted, and roasted in a 300°F oven for 45 minutes.

ROOT VEGETABLE SOUPS

As long as you've gone to the trouble to roast the vegetables, don't forget they transform easily into wonderful soups. Puree in a standing blender, or use an immersion blender or food processor. *SERVES 6*

1 onion, chopped
2 tablespoons olive oil
1 recipe Roasted Winter
  Vegetables (previous page)

1 quart chicken stock
½ cup heavy cream
Salt and freshly ground black
  pepper

In a large skillet, sauté the onion in the olive oil until soft, about 10 minutes. Add the roasted vegetables and cook for about 7 minutes, to meld the flavors. Pour the stock over the vegetables and bring to a boil, then reduce the heat and simmer for 20 minutes.

Using a blender or food processor, puree until completely smooth. Stir in the cream and bring to a simmer; season with salt and pepper if necessary. Serve with croutons or crispy fried shallots.

ROLLING PIN   Both Deans own several rolling pins. In a pinch, faced without one in an under-equipped kitchen, we've even been known to employ an empty wine bottle. When purchasing a rolling pin, the simpler the better. Dean Pollak was presented with a high-tech model and after many expletives she decided there was one use for it: clocking the inventor in the head. The handles and the roller did not move together so the roller just spun in situ without flattening the dough.

"A blast of refrigerated air is no friend to baked goods."

PIE DOUGH

A homemade pie says "I love you" and we can never say that often enough to our family and friends. We want everyone to stop thinking they have to purchase pie dough. We want you to try making pastry at least four times before you throw in the towel. Flour and butter only cost a few cents to experiment with while you are learning. After a few attempts you will wonder why you held out so long. And if you are not happy, roll and cut your first tries into crackers or cookies and sprinkle with cheese or sugar, depending on what you feel like eating.

    If you are going to make homemade piecrust, our preference for baking is a glass pie pan. Glass evenly distributes heat and facilitates a crisp, flaky crust. The Deans never add sugar to our dough because we like the contrast of savory crust and sweet filling. ***MAKES ONE 9-INCH PIECRUST***

1½ cups unbleached
all-purpose flour
1½ sticks (6 ounces) unsalted
butter, cold, cut into
4 pieces
3 to 4 tablespoons ice water

Preheat the oven to 450°F.

METHOD 1/BY MACHINE Using a food processor or standing mixer, beat the flour with the cold butter until large, pea-size lumps form.

Now, begin to add the ice water 1 tablespoon at a time, until the dough just begins to come together. Do not wait until a ball forms or the dough will be tough. Turn off the mixer and reach in the bowl to pinch some dough together. If it holds together, the dough is finished.

Transfer the dough to a large sheet of wax paper and gather up the sides, pushing the dough into a ball. Place the wax-paper-covered ball in the freezer while you make the pie filling.

Roll out the chilled dough between 2 pieces of wax paper until the dough is two inches larger than your pie pan, roughly 12 inches in diameter. Peel one piece of waxed paper off the dough and flip the dough into the pie pan; remove the top layer of wax paper. Lightly press the dough into the pan and crimp the edges. Do not worry if the edges are not perfect—this is a homemade pie and should look like one.

To partially bake the piecrust: Put a fresh layer of wax paper on top of the dough and fill with 1½ cups dried beans, raw rice, or pie weights. Bake for 10 minutes, then remove the paper and weights and poke the bottom of the crust with a fork several times. Return the piecrust to the oven for another 8 minutes for a partially cooked pie shell. (For a fully cooked pie shell, return to the oven for 16 minutes.)

METHOD 2/BY HAND Place the flour in a medium bowl. Using a pastry blender or two knives, cut the butter into the flour. When the mixture forms very large, pea-size lumps, with chunks of butter still visible, add 3 tablespoons ice water. Stir with a rubber spatula. You will need to add up to 3 more tablespoons water to get the dough to form a shaggy mass. When the dough has almost come together, spoon it onto a large sheet of wax paper, or into a gallon-size resealable plastic bag. Gather up the edges of the wax paper or plastic bag to force the dough into a smooth ball. The paper and the bag keep your counter clean. Refrigerate the covered dough to let the dough, and you, take a little rest, at least 30 minutes. Now, proceed with rolling the dough as before.

ACADEMY PIES

Choosing which pie recipe to include in our book has been the most difficult decision we have ever made. What pie don't we love? Rhubarb? Apple? Cherry? Our very favorite ones tend to be the fruit-filled pies, but that hardly narrowed our choices down. We realize we will have to dedicate an entire book to pies, but until then we are choosing two pies for this book: Peach Pie because our home state, South Carolina, produces more peaches than Georgia (so ha!) and Coconut Pie as a wink and a nod to the trade that connected Charleston and Barbados during the eighteenth century and the resulting coconuts imported when Charleston was incorporated.

PEACH PIE

We don't consider peach pie a dessert—for us it's a breakfast food. If you have any doubt that our assertion is correct, we charge you with making a peach pie (and somehow you and your family members forgetting about it after dinner—good luck), and the next morning everyone having coffee and a slice of peach pie for breakfast. *MAKES ONE 9-INCH PIE*

8 to 9 peaches (about 3 pounds), peeled, pitted, and thinly sliced
½ cup sugar, plus 1 tablespoon for sprinkling
1 tablespoon cornstarch
Juice of 1 lemon

¼ teaspoon salt
½ teaspoon almond extract
1 cup blackberries (optional)
2 recipes Pie Dough (previous page)

Mix the peach slices with the rest of the ingredients except the pie dough and reserved tablespoon of sugar, stirring with a rubber spatula until all traces of the cornstarch disappear.

Roll out half of the pie dough and place it in a 9-inch glass pie pan. Trim the edge and refrigerate while rolling out the other half of the dough for the top. Roll it into an 11-inch round.

Fill the pie shell with the peaches, mounding the center slightly. Place the second round of dough on top of the peaches, tucking the overhang under the bottom crust. Crimp the border with your fingers. Cover the pie with plastic wrap and refrigerate for 1 hour or overnight.

Preheat the oven to 425°F.

Slash the top pastry in four or five places with a knife and sprinkle the top with the 1 tablespoon of sugar. Bake the pie on the bottom rack of the oven for 50 minutes. If the dough darkens around the edges too much, cover with a piece of foil.

Let the pie cool for 2 to 4 hours. For breakfast eating, cover the cooled pie with wax paper and hide it in kitchen until morning.

COCONUT PIE

This pie is over-the-top delicious. The bourbon is the Deans' secret ingredient, so please do not tell your friends that we spike their desserts. Let's keep it between us. *MAKES ONE 9-INCH PIE*

3 eggs
1 cup sugar
1 cup unsweetened coconut
　　flakes

½ teaspoon salt
2 to 3 tablespoons bourbon
One 9-inch pie shell, partially
　　baked (see page 35)

Preheat the oven to 325°F.

In a large bowl, thoroughly whisk together all the ingredients except the pie shell. Pour into the partially baked pie shell and bake for 30 minutes. Let the pie cool for at least 20 minutes before serving. This pie is fantastic warm or at room temperature, but we have not tasted it cold, because we have never had leftovers.

PASTRY OR DOUGH SCRAPER The Deans use their pastry scrapers in two ways. Dean Pollak uses hers for cutting dough into the correct portions, such as for English Muffins (page 169) or pizza dough. This tool slices through dough more easily than a conventional blade. Dean Manigault really enjoys using her scraper for cleanup—scraping off excess dough from her countertop when she has finished cooking.

GRAPEFRUIT KNIFE Dean Manigault's jaw dropped when she found out that Dean Pollak did not even know that grapefruit knives existed. Dean Manigault starts every day by separating each section of her grapefruit with this indispensable tool. If you don't know what one is, it is a small knife with a serrated edge all the way around the blade, including its slightly curved tip. This is to get under and around each segment of a halved grapefruit.

DISH TOWELS You can't have too many of these. They are fun to collect and good to give as house gifts. There's nothing these linens can't do. You can roll up just-washed lettuce leaves in clean dish towels and store in the refrigerator to keep the lettuce at its peak of freshness. You can use dish towels as pot holders, counter wipers, or dish dryers. Dampened dish towels create a non-slip countertop surface for items placed on top, they can be inserted under linen tablecloths to provide steam when ironing, and they can cover a bowl of dough to prevent the dough from drying out. Dish towels are almost as versatile as the kitchens in which they are housed.

BASIC SKILLS:

The ABCs of Cooking

Perhaps a roadblock to your spending more time in your kitchen is that some of the language used in cookbooks is unknown to you. If you don't fully understand the instructions, then you have no idea how incredibly easy it can be to execute them. If you know the following terms and techniques, you've got the basics covered.

"The ABCs of Cooking."

SYLLABUS

BLANCH

Who among us isn't improved by a quick plunge in a hot tub?

DEFINITION: *to scald briefly in water as a preparatory step for an ingredient.*

BRAISE

Still waters run deep. Sometimes it takes time and patience to
coax the best out of a tough nut.

DEFINITION: *to brown in fat, then simmer in liquid to cook through.*

BRINE

A little work on the front end can create extraordinary results on the back end.

DEFINITION: *to immerse or preserve in salty water.*

FRY

Bubble, bubble, toil and trouble. Beware, once you've mastered this art, you might
not want to eat any other way, health benefits be damned.

DEFINITION: *to shallow- or deep-cook in hot oil.*

POACH

For those with a delicate constitution, a leisurely soak in an herb-infused broth
is what's needed to get table-ready.

DEFINITION: *to cook gently in simmering liquid.*

RISE

Only Superman himself will be able to jump over these creations in a single bound
once they have risen to their full height. Be patient.

DEFINITION: *to let leavening increase a food's height, size, or volume.*

SAUTÉ

The technique just sounds delicious.

DEFINITION: *to cook food through quickly in a skillet over high, direct heat.*

SEAR

Every caveman knew that high heat creates the crunchiest crust contrasted with
the rarest insides. Go ahead and satisfy your inner beast.

DEFINITION: *to brown the exterior of meat quickly over high, direct heat.*

BLANCHING

Springtime always puts the Deans in the mood for blanching. Baby vegetables are at their peak and only require a touch of heat to bring out their maximum flavor. For these spring vegetables, any more time in water would be a travesty, as opposed to their enormous, elderly wintertime relatives, which need more cooking on the stove or in the oven to break them down a bit. After the brief blanch, a quick plunge in an ice bath ensures the vegetables retain their vibrant color, because the cooking process is halted. Then they can be rewarmed in a pan sauce or eaten at room temperature.

----- c -----

BEAN AMANDINE

We just couldn't help ourselves. The Deans spied a newly married acquaintance of ours with a large bag of green beans in the supermarket, so we asked her what was on her dinner party menu. No party, she said, she was only buying beans for her husband and herself. We realized she was clueless about portion size. Thank goodness the Deans were on the spot to rescue her and instruct on how to take the guesswork out of buying beans. No math involved. Pick out a handful of beans to feed one person, two handfuls feed two people, a few more means enough for seconds. Class dismissed.

SERVES 4 TO 6

1 pound mixed green, yellow, and purple beans, trimmed

$2/3$ cup toasted slivered almonds

2 tablespoons butter

Blanch the beans in boiling, lightly salted water for 45 seconds. Drain immediately in a colander and give them a quick cold-water rinse.

In a small skillet, sauté the almonds in the butter over medium-high heat until brown, about 3 minutes. Add the drained beans to the pan with the toasted almonds and sauté until the beans are cooked to the optimal crispness, 4 to 8 minutes. Serve immediately.

BRAISING

You are going to encounter some tough guys in the kitchen: the connective tissue in inexpensive cuts of meat. But that's why there's braising! Never use expensive lean cuts of meat when braising. Not only do they not taste better, they just fall apart because they do not have enough sinew to withstand long, low-temperature cooking. Only time can wear down the collagen and turn it into toothsome gelatin, which adds body to the sauce and tenderizes the meat.

BOEUF BOURGUIGNON

No one can be surprised to learn that the Deans differ on what we serve with our stews. Dean Pollak has the problem of filling her children's stomachs, so she often adds sautéed small roasted potatoes to the stew and then ladles the stew over buttered egg noodles. A double starch gut bomb has kept her from having to serve a second dinner two hours later. Dean Manigault has a whole different set of issues. She has two young girls whose appetites are like those of epiphytes in a humid hothouse. A few tablespoons of stew over a well-buttered piece of toast occasionally gets past their lips and gums, even if only by accident. One pot of stew can last her the entire winter.

For special occasions, such as shameless brownnosing of VIPs, Dean Manigaut sautés chanterelles and adds them at the last minute. When Dean Pollak gets her hands on chanterelles, she sautés them and eats them herself. White mushrooms are more than adequate for her guests. Besides, for her three enormous sons, there are not enough chanterelles on the planet to feed them, even if they cost nothing, which they decidedly do not.
SERVES 6

¾ cup flour, for dredging

Salt and freshly ground black
pepper

2 pounds beef chuck or round,
cut into 1½- to 2-inch cubes

5 tablespoons olive oil

8 leeks, white part only, cut in
half lengthwise, thoroughly
rinsed, and cut crosswise
¼ inch thick

¾ pound carrots, cut in half
lengthwise and cut cross-
wise ¼ inch thick

1 bottle robust red wine

One 8-ounce package
demi-glace (found in the
freezer section of gourmet
stores)

10 whole black peppercorns

3 or 4 sprigs fresh thyme, or 1½
teaspoons dried thyme

1½ cups water

A handful of chanterelles or
morels (optional)

1 tablespoon butter

1 handful chopped fresh
flat-leaf parsley

The first thing you need to do is season your flour with a little salt and pepper on a plate. Coat the beef in the flour. In a large pot with a lid, such as a Dutch oven, heat 2 tablespoons of the olive oil over medium-high heat. When the oil is hot but not smoking, add the meat, a few cubes at a time, to cover the bottom of the pan without touching. You will have to work in batches. You are creating a crust of the flour on the outside of the beef. Once browned on one side, flip the beef over with tongs and brown the other side, about 4 minutes per side. Transfer all the meat to a platter. Pour out any excess grease, but do not clean the bottom of the pan. Add the remaining 3 table-spoons olive oil. All those browned bits are going to add to the flavor of your stew. Heat the oil until hot and add the leeks and carrots. Let them sweat for 10 minutes, until softened but not browned, stirring every 2 minutes from the bottom of the pan up to evenly distribute the oil and prevent burning.

Return the beef to the pot. Add the wine, demi-glace, peppercorns, thyme, and water. This may seem like a lot of liquid but when you serve the stew with egg noodles, toasted bread, or mashed potatoes, there cannot be too much gravy. Set to a low simmer and cook for at least 2 hours, skimming foam off of the top every so often.

You can make the stew a day

ahead and refrigerate it but at the very least, let it come to room temperature before reheating and serving. Flavors seem to become infinitely more complex when a long-stewed item gets chilled before it gets reheated. The alchemy is a mystery to Dean Manigualt, but the proof is in the flavor. The stew can also be frozen for up to a month.

Just before serving, in a small saucepan or skillet, heat the mushrooms over medium-high heat in the butter until their liquid is released. Add to the pot of stew or sprinkle onto individual servings, along with the parsley.

BRINING

Brining is where the Deans part ways. Now we will share our respective secrets.

———— ❦ ————

DEAN MANIGAULT'S DRY BRINE

It's the simplest thing ever: sea salt and freshly ground black pepper. Then refrigerate the brined food. That's it! The salt adds incomparable flavor and the dry refrigerator air will ensure a good caramelized sear for meat and crisp skin for poultry. Note: If brining with salt in advance, you will want less salt at the table.

FOR BIG CUTS OF MEAT:
Sprinkle sea salt and pepper all over. Cover loosely with wax paper, and refrigerate for a few hours, or overnight.

FOR WHOLE CHICKENS:
Wash and dry thoroughly. Sprinkle sea salt all over. Stuff cavity with a mass of parsley. Loosely cover with wax paper and refrigerate overnight.

DEAN POLLAK'S WET BRINE

The basic ratio is $1/3$ cup salt to 1 quart water. You can also add ¼ cup sugar and any spices you like. Wet brining guarantees moist, tender meat. Besides intensifying flavor, the salt plumps up muscle fibers, allowing them to absorb more water and stay juicy when cooked. Turkeys prefer to relax in brine for 24 to 48 hours; whole chickens and cuts of pork can bathe for 1 to 4 hours. Never wet brine lamb or beef.

FRYING

The Deans like the temperamental nature of frying, because it adds excitement to any meal. Not too much, mind you—the Deans are not drama queens. Frying has a long history in the Southeast: We ask, is there anyone in the world who doesn't like fried chicken? This cooking technique creates a crispy crust, which yields to a toothsomely succulent interior.

We will hold your hand the first time, since there are a few things you have to know. Frying will create a big mess in your kitchen, and the aroma of the fried foods can linger, so keep your kitchen well ventilated. Invest in a deep-fat thermometer, because if the oil is at too low a temperature, it will seep into the food, and if the oil is too hot, the coating will burn before the interior cooks through. A thermometer, clipped to the side of your cauldron, lets you know the temperature of your oil at all times.

FRIED ZUCCHINI

How many children delight at being served a plate of zucchini? None. How many children will eat fried zucchini? All. Fried zucchini tastes better than French fries—and is less starchy to boot. A simple flour-and-water batter turns into an irresistible crispy cloud encasing the zucchini sticks. *SERVES 4 TO 6*

1 cup water
2/3 cup unbleached all-purpose
    flour

1 pound zucchini, sliced
    lengthwise 1/8 inch thick and
    2 inches long
Vegetable oil, for frying
Salt

In a shallow bowl, whisk together the water and flour. The batter should have the consistency of sour cream. Adjust your measurements accordingly.

Into a Dutch oven or stock pot, over high heat, pour enough oil to come 3/4 inch up the side of the pot. When the oil reaches 375°F, dip the zucchini slices in the batter. Transfer to the hot oil one handful at a time, so as not to crowd the pan. Flip a couple of times until the zucchini are golden brown all over. Your oil must be hot enough so the cooking is finished within 2 to 3 minutes. Sprinkle with salt and serve piping hot with homemade mayonnaise or rémoulade (see pages 28 and 49).

POACHING

When time is not the issue but presentation is, the Deans poach. Poaching is one of the most elegant of the culinary arts. An evening spent in a warm bath creates an entirely different texture than one spent in a hot oven. Poached foods have no crisp charred bits; everything is silky smooth. Do not let the gentle simmer put you to sleep. Poaching can be deceiving. Overcooking is a real possibility, so do not trust anyone, even master chef Paul Bocuse. Dean Pollak is still ruing the overcooked tenderloin she served at a dinner party, following Monsieur Bocuse's directions to the letter. Instead, use an instant-read thermometer to check the internal temperature of the meat and reduce the risk of a nasty surprise when you slice into the cooked meat.

BEEF ON A STRING

Everyone has seen poached salmon, and what an impressive sight it is. But have you ever seen poached beef tenderloin? We want to change that. You will feel like Opie and Sheriff Taylor when you tug on the string and pull out your six- to eight-pound dinner. Fish on!!!

Don't be shy about adding vegetables (mushrooms, baby squash, pearl onions, or cabbage), sausage (duck or garlicky pork), or marrow bones (find them in the freezer section of some supermarkets) to the poaching stock. Poached tenderloin is delicious served with rémoulade sauce and/or horseradish sauce (see page 49). These sauces are equally good—be sure to make both of them. They'll keep, refrigerated, for a week. *SERVES 6*

3 quarts water or chicken,
beef, or veal stock
½ pound carrots, cut into
matchsticks
½ pound small new potatoes,
one strip peeled from
center of each
6 leeks, white part only
2 ribs celery
One 28-ounce can whole
canned tomatoes, prefera-
bly San Marzano, with liquid
1 onion, halved, each half
studded with 3 cloves

1 sprig each parsley, chervil,
and tarragon
2 tablespoons coarse salt
1 teaspoon whole black
peppercorns
4 pounds beef filet, trimmed
and tied
12 medium Academy Croutons
(see page 32)
½ cup grated Parmesan
Coarse mustard, cornichons,
and small pickled onions,
for serving

In a large pot, bring the water to a boil. Add everything but the beef, croutons, cheese, and garnishes. Lower the heat and simmer for 20 minutes.

Tie a piece of kitchen string to the tied beef, and secure it to the handle of the pot; this will help in removing the meat. Plunge the beef into the poaching liquid and simmer for 20 minutes, skimming the surface of the liquid occasionally. Remove the beef from the pot and test the temperature with an instant-read thermometer. The Deans like to pull out our tenderloin at 125°F for medium-rare (the internal temperature will keep climbing for a few minutes and will reach 130°F). Let rest for at least 10 and up to 40 minutes. Do not remove the strings during the resting period.

While the beef is resting, sprinkle the cheese on the croutons and broil for 2 minutes until the cheese is melted, but be careful not to burn it.

Serve the meat on a platter surrounded by the vegetables, croutons, mustard, cornichons, and pickled onions. Remove the string just before slicing the meat. The leftover beef, coarsely chopped, is fantastic mixed with the rémoulade sauce.

SAUCE RÉMOULADE

MAKES 1 CUP

1 cup mayonnaise

2 tablespoons capers

1 tablespoon pickled green
    peppercorns, drained

6 cornichons, finely chopped

3 tablespoons chopped
    fresh parsley

2 tablespoons chopped
    fresh chervil

2 to 3 tablespoons chopped
    fresh tarragon

2 to 3 teaspoons anchovy
    paste (Dean Pollak likes 2
    teaspoons of anchovy paste,
    Dean Manigault likes 3 and
    isn't ruling out 4; add anchovy
    paste in increments so you
    can be your own judge)

In a bowl, mix together all the
ingredients. Store in the refrigerator
for up to 1 week.

HORSERADISH SAUCE

MAKES 1 CUP

2 tomatoes

¾ cup crème fraîche

2 heaping teaspoons
    prepared horseradish

Pinch of salt

In a pot of simmering water, blanch
the tomatoes, then peel and seed
them. Transfer to a saucepan and
cook over low heat for 15 to 20
minutes to evaporate the juices.

Stir in the crème fraîche,
horseradish, and salt. Store in the
refrigerator for up to 1 week.

RISING

Rising in the kitchen happens from morning through night. The first things to rise are your eyelids and mood with that first cup of coffee. Sometimes, in order to get our motors running at maximum efficiency, the Deans' coffee resembles crude oil in consistency. A little satin bathrobe can also be a mood lifter.

Other risers in the kitchen may not be so personal but their effects are no less dramatic. A myriad of ingredients cause risings to occur. Air, baking powder, yeast, and eggs are all leavening ingredients. Their inclusion in a recipe signals dramatic things to come.

Any rising is based on a chemical reaction. Even if you flunked chemistry in high school, it's not too late to get your PhD in the kitchen. The majesty of a rising soufflé can make you feel as brilliant as a tenured physics professor.

DEANS' CLIFFNOTES FOR SOUFFLÉS

Eggs do more in the kitchen than anyone else. These little guys are literally the glue that holds everything together. Creating custards and soufflés may sound daunting but we can assure you these are learnable skills that you should have.

TO SEPARATE EGG YOLKS from whites with ease, start with cold eggs. After separating, return the yolks to the refrigerator and let the whites sit on the countertop to come to room temperature. The cold temperature keeps the yolks from breaking when separating, while the room temperature encourages the whites to rise high when whipped.

FOR THE BEST WHIPPING HEIGHT, use older eggs rather than fresh ones.

IF USING AN ELECTRIC MIXER, whisk the egg whites on low speed and increase the speed gradually. If you want a great exercise for your arms, whip by hand.

ADD A PINCH of cream of tartar after one minute of whipping to help egg whites hold their volume.

START ADDING ANY SUGAR in a thin stream the moment soft peaks appear. Sugar added all at once will deflate the egg whites.

BEAT THE WHITES to soft, not stiff, peaks. Overly whipped whites do not fold smoothly into their base. Underbeating is better than overbeating.

SEAT YOUR GUESTS five minutes before a first-course soufflé, so the presentation is at its maximum height.

PUT A DESSERT SOUFFLÉ in the oven ten minutes after you serve a main course.

IF DISASTER STRIKES, describe a fallen soufflé as your grandmother's pudding recipe.

CHEESE SOUFFLÉ

Soufflé making is a right of passage at the Academy. We can see our students' confidence rising right along with the soufflés. Even if the rest of the day was a total disaster, the Deans get a frisson when our oven door opens to reveal a puffy golden cheese excitement. To make a soufflé for two (for those marital moments) halve all ingredients, use 3 egg yolks, 5 egg whites, and 1 cup shredded cheese. *SERVES 4*

3 tablespoons unsalted butter,
    plus 1 tablespoon butter
    softened
¼ cup grated Parmesan
¼ cup flour
1 cup whole milk
½ teaspoon salt
½ teaspoon freshly ground
    black pepper
¼ teaspoon cayenne

1 serrano pepper, halved,
    seeded, finally chopped
1 bunch chives, snipped
7 medium egg yolks
9 medium egg whites
8 ounces Gruyére (Deans'
    favorite) or cheddar,
    coarsely shredded,
    or goat cheese, about
    2 cups, crumbled

Preheat the oven to 375°F.

Butter a 2-quart soufflé dish with the 1 tablespoon softened butter. Sprinkle 2 tablespoons Parmesan inside the dish.

In a medium saucepan, melt the remaining 3 tablespoons butter over medium-low heat. Whisk in the flour to make a roux, whisking constantly for 2 to 3 minutes. (Use a flat whisk if you own one, made especially to get into the corners of the pan.) Stirring constantly, slowly add the milk, and bring to a low boil. Whisk for 2 minutes until the sauce is thick. Remove from the heat; season with the salt, black pepper, and cayenne. Whisk in the egg yolks and stir in the shredded or crumbled cheese.

Using an electric mixer, beat the egg whites and a pinch of salt at medium-high speed until frothy. Increase the speed to high and beat until stiff peaks form. With a rubber spatula, fold one quarter of the whites into the yolk base until no

"The most heated 'marital moment' will dissipate in the presence of a cheesy soufflé."

streaks remain. Then fold in the rest of the egg whites, being careful not to overblend. A few white streaks are not a problem.

Spoon the mixture into the prepared dish. Smooth the surface with an offset spatula and sprinkle the remaining 2 tablespoons Parmesan on top. Bake in the bottom third of the oven until golden brown and puffed, about 35 minutes. We prefer a soft interior. Serve at once with a tart green salad. The most elegant lunch or dinner on the planet.

Sautéing is the go-to method most often employed by the Deans. This is not a do-ahead technique. The second the food hits the pan, your meal is almost ready, and tasty it is, too. The entire process is done on the stovetop so the food needs to be thin enough to cook through while sautéing. This technique is great for scaloppini, schnitzel, hamburgers, and vegetables.

There is nobody who cannot master sautéing within one week. The process is quick so there is no opportunity to get distracted by other kitchen activities. Action is happening right before your eyes, not hidden in an oven or under a lid. If cooking is not going fast enough, turn the heat up; if it's going too fast, turn the heat down, or take the pan off the burner for a moment.

CRISPY SALMON

This is no time to penny pinch. When you see fresh filleted Atlantic salmon, jump all over it. Your main course is ready in ten minutes and tastier than anything you've eaten in five years. The clarifying of the butter is almost half the recipe but it is an essential step because it can tolerate a much higher temperature than regular butter without burning. Detention is in order for diners who neglect to eat the crispy skin. You are not too old to wear a dunce cap.

Salt

Freshly ground black pepper

Flour, for coating

6 ounces fresh Atlantic salmon
   fillets (1 per guest)

Clarified butter (recipe
   follows), 1 tablespoon
   per fillet

Preheat the broiler. Season the salmon with salt and pepper and then dredge it in flour just to coat. In a large skillet, heat the butter over high heat. Add the salmon and sear until the skin is quite crisp. Place the skillet under the broiler for 5 to 10 minutes, depending on the thickness of the fillet. Watch closely for browning because the broiler can turn things from brown to black in an instant, and always while your attention is diverted.

CLARIFIED BUTTER

To clarify butter, melt a stick of unsalted butter in a small saucepan over low heat. The butter will separate, with the milk solids remaining on the bottom of the pan. (This is why you want a small saucepan: If the butter spreads out in a large pan, you will not be able to skim the top.) Remove the bright clear yellow emulsion, being sure that the white bits remain behind (they are what burn). Indians call clarified butter ghee and keep it in their refrigerator all the time. You do the same: Refrigerate any unused clarified butter for future use.

SEARING

Searing brings out our caveman instincts. We don a leopard-print blouse, put a bone in our hair, and start cooking meat over ridiculously high temperatures. The effect is immediate and dramatic. When sautéing, we want a golden-brown color; when we sear, we're aiming for a dark-brown, caramelized crust, with abundant crispy bits left in the pan. The remnants should not be wasted. Adding a touch of wine and cream and scraping them up with a wooden spoon creates an easy and delicious pan sauce every time.

SCALLOPS

Large diver scallops are perfect for quick searing. When the top and bottom get caramelized and golden brown, they are sweet and salty, rich and meaty, all at once. If you've gone to the trouble to buy enormous expensive sea scallops, then follow the next two tips: Never crowd them in your pan, and you must cook them briefly over high heat to achieve a crust without overcooking them. *SERVES 4*

4 tablespoons clarified butter (above)	1 lemon, quartered
1 pound large diver sea scallops	

In a medium nonstick skillet, heat 2 tablespoons of the clarified butter over high heat. Add half the scallops in a single layer, not crowding the pan. Cook for about 2 minutes per side. If too much liquid is released, immediately remove a few of the scallops from the pan, otherwise they will braise and not get a crust. Cook the remaining scallops in the remaining clarified butter. Serve with the lemon wedges.

We Will Get Through This Together

One of the best-kept secrets of a well-run home is the role everyday cooking plays in anchoring a family. The kitchen is the place, and dinner is the time, to create an environment of relaxation and love. Dinner is the mainstay of family life. If you are a parent, this is your time to do prime intel gathering, as well as to expand your family's culinary tastes. The Deans know from experience that over an extended period of time, cooking and eating together on a regular basis around a kitchen or dining room table nurtures family relationships and establishes a foundation for lifelong intimacy. When you are sad and blue is when you most feel like ditching this routine, but now is actually the time you should redouble your effort. The Deans have some strategies to get you through the tough times.

CRUSH THE BOREDOM

The Deans' number one thought on boredom is that boredom breeds boredom. If you approach cooking as a drudgery and a nuisance, none of your meals will be tasty. There are as many ways to approach daily cooking as there are meals to serve. Your perspective is the issue. You have not been relegated to endless KP duty; instead you are the general in charge of solidifying family bonds and improving overall quality of life for the people you love best, starting with yourself. Dean Manigault's daughter, India, maintains that a good habit can become permanent after seventeen consecutive days of strict adherence. The day you are ready to begin, mark you calendar and make a firm commitment to cook at least one meal a day for the next seventeen. After you have done this, you'll find yourself easing into and enjoying meal preparation. By making daily cooking a habit instead of a chore, you minimize the stress. The ritual of planning, shopping, setting the table, and cooking the meal essentially stays the same. Any kind of repetitive rote movement is a meditation. Cooking is no different.

"Transported back to St. Croix without having to brave customs lines"

How do you think Cal Ripken, who played with the Baltimore Orioles for twenty-one years and in 2,632 successive games, kept fresh? The Deans bet that he accomplished this feat by treating every game as an individual event and used each as an opportunity to prove his prowess. By doing something over and over again, you can relax into the task and relish the changing nuances. In a short time, you will tap into your creative juices. Once you've mastered a basic recipe, curiosity can start to take over and you are free to wonder, for instance, *Shall I use lemon instead of garlic?* And since this is your time of creativity, there is no wrong answer. Do not let one or two botched meals throw you off your task. Cal Ripken did not hit a home run every time at bat.

Occasionally, even the Deans don't feel creative. That's when we pull out our most-used recipes. After years of daily cooking, we have mastered many recipes that don't require any brainwork on our part. Then, branching out a little, we keep fresh nightly by taking the recipes we know best and adding or subtracting steps or ingredients based on what is in our refrigerator, what's at the farmers' market, what's on sale, or what's on our minds. Once in a while, we need new ideas to get energized, so we cook our way through a particular cookbook or food magazine.

Dean Manigault sometimes enlists the help of her children to spice things up. Just being told what to cook can trigger an idea or expand the repertoire. On a recent visit to see her daughter Caroline, Dean Pollak remembered what fun it can be to cook breakfast for dinner. She also loved how Caroline snuck in vegetables under the cheese in a frittata for her two- and four-year-old daughters.

Remember, too, that children and spouses can be enlisted for hands-on labor. At first everyone may balk at a bit of extra work, but at the end of the seventeen days, everyone will have fallen into line. One night a week children over the age of twelve can be put in charge of the family meal preparation and the parents of the cleanup. Make one night family night and cook together. Try a meal of tapas around the coffee table, with everyone picking out one dish.

You can use your kitchen as a time machine. Create recipes that remind you of trips you have taken. A vacation to Cane Garden in St. Croix (the Deans *do* occasionally rest) had us cooking rice in coconut milk and sprinkling virtually everything with fresh hot peppers. We weren't changing the entire upholstery of our cooking, just adding new throw pillows. We've long known that putting lemons in the cavity of a chicken was a home run, but slipping orange slices under the skin seasoned the dish in a whole new way. The orange flavor was more potent then we had imagined possible and fit the tropical mood we were in. Taking the recipe home with us was a way of extending the vacation. On a cold winter night, we can now serve orange chicken, coconut rice and a rum drink and the family will be transported back to St. Croix without the price of airline tickets or having to brave customs lines.

CHICKEN CANE GARDEN

Citrus and chicken go hand in hand. Be sure to slice the oranges as thinly as possible. Carefully separate the chicken skin from the meat with your fingers. Go slow—you don't want to tear the skin. Load from the back up: Slip in the first orange slice as far as you can, all the way to the thighs, and then work your way forward. You probably will be able to fit two or three slices on each half of the chicken. Stuff the cavity with the remaining oranges slices. (If you plan ahead, refrigerate the chicken, uncovered, for an hour or so, for extra flavor and crispness.) When the chicken emerges fully cooked from the oven, its crisp skin is punctuated by the citrus medallions within. *SERVES 4*

One 4 to 5½ pound whole
    chicken, well rinsed
Coarse salt and freshly ground
    black pepper
1 orange, halved
1 whole head garlic, halved

    crosswise
5 tablespoons butter
1 tablespoon olive oil
1 to 2 tablespoons water or
    Grand Marnier

Pat the chicken dry. Season the chicken with salt and pepper inside and out. Thinly slice one half of the orange. Slip the orange slices in a single layer under the chicken skin, covering the breasts and thighs. Place the other half of the orange in the cavity of the chicken along with the garlic and 2 tablespoons butter.

Preheat the oven to 450°F. In a medium ovenproof skillet, heat the remaining 3 tablespoons butter and the olive oil over medium-high heat. When the butter is melted, add the chicken and cook for 5 minutes on each side, until golden brown.

Put the pan, with the chicken breast side up, in the oven and roast until crisp, 60 to 75 minutes, basting about every 15 minutes. Test for doneness by piercing the chicken leg—the juices should run clear. Transfer the chicken to a cutting board and carve.

Squeeze the cooked orange from the chicken's cavity into the skillet with 1 to 2 tablespoons of the water or Grand Marnier and simmer on low heat for 2 minutes. Pour the sauce over the chicken.

"Rice to South Carolinians is like pasta to Italians."

COCONUT RICE

Rice to South Carolinians is like pasta to Italians: essential to our well-being. We love every type of rice and have tried all kinds for this recipe. Surprisingly, they all work! *SERVES 3 TO 4*

1½ cups water
1 cup basmati jasmine rice
1 teaspoon sea salt

1 15-ounce can full-fat coconut milk, well shaken

Preheat the oven to 400°F.

In a medium saucepan, bring the water to a boil. Add the rice and salt. Return the water to a boil, then reduce the heat, cover, and simmer for 2 minutes less than the package directions, 15 to 16 minutes.

Spoon the rice into a shallow glass baking dish. Pour the coconut milk on top and stir. Bake for 20 minutes. Convert the oven from bake to broil. Run the rice under the broiler until golden brown. Don't take your eye off of it (keep the oven door ajar) until it is crisp.

MAKE-AHEAD MEALS

In times of peace, prepare for war. A freezer stocked full of delicious foods when you are feeling good will be a lifesaver when you are tired or pressed for time. Spread the labor out over a manageable period of time. Stews made of tough cuts of meat can be cooked while you sleep. Long-simmering pasta sauces can be made ahead and stored in the freezer, waiting to be married to the pasta at the final moment. If you're feeling particularly energetic, you can whip up two meals at once and save one for the future. The Deans assure you that with a few of these do-ahead dishes and a well-stocked pantry of essentials, you'll be able to walk in the door and create a tasty meal right off the bat.

OXTAIL STEW

This recipe separates the wheat from the chaff, and the men from the boys. Some of you are going to read this and think "I am going to do this tomorrow" and some of you will think "This is the stupidest thing I have ever heard in my life, as well as the most disgusting." Clearly we are writing for the former group, not the latter. This recipe does its initial cooking while you sleep. If that is not multitasking, then we are not Deans. We work even while we sleep.

Serve this stew over creamy mashed potatoes, toss it with pasta, or spoon it over buttered toast; top it with a gremolata (see page 28).

SERVES 6 TO 8

10 pounds oxtails, sliced into
  rounds
Salt and freshly ground black
  pepper
Flour, for coating

2½ pounds onions, sliced
2 whole heads garlic, halved
1½ to 2 bottles red wine
Glace or demi-glace de veau

Heat the oven to 250°F.

Season the oxtails with salt and pepper and coat in flour. In a large Dutch oven, sauté the oxtails over medium-high heat. Your goal is a golden-brown crust on both the oxtails and the bottom of the pan, because the crust is where the flavor lies. As the oxtails are done, transfer them to a plate while you continue cooking the others.

Return the oxtails to the pot and top with the onions and garlic. Pour in enough red wine to come within ½ inch of the top of the pot. Cover with the lid. On your way to bed, place the pot in the hot oven. Sleep your requisite 8 hours.

Wake up. Remove the pot from the oven. Transfer the meat and onions to a baking dish and the liquid to a bowl. Refrigerate for several hours.

Now comes the fun part. Let your fingers be your guides. Separate the meat in tiny little chunks from the sinew and bones. Any piece you do not want to put in your mouth, because it is too fatty or sinewy, discard. There will be a lot of refuse. Keep all the onions with the meat and squeeze the garlic pulp from the skins onto the meat.

Skim all the fat from the sauce. Put the defatted sauce, meat, onions, and garlic in a large saucepan. Bring to a boil, and stir in the glace de veau. If the sauce seems too thick, add a bit more red wine. If the sauce is too thin, simmer until it thickens.

"*This is the STUPIDEST thing I have ever heard in my life, as well as the most DISGUSTING.*"

"A meal you could proudly serve to a James Beard Award–winning chef,
if one happened to drop by."

TIME-DEFYING MEALS

Who decided that 20 or 30 minutes is the Holy Grail timing for preparing dinner? When we are tired, the Deans want to get something cooking within two minutes, not twenty. And, like all people, just because we don't feel like doing something doesn't mean we don't have to do it. When we have been long at work and we come home and our families look like a nest of baby birds with their beaks open, and it's our job to feed them—these are the days we wonder who had these children, and why? Who knew when we brought that precious bundle home from the hospital that we were committing ourselves to twenty-five years of nightly cooking? These are the days we need the quickest meals possible.

SAUSAGE SUPPER

Since our larder is stocked, we pull out a can of tomato sauce and a package of sausage—but not just any old sausage. There are wonderful artisanal sausages and we keep a variety in our freezers at all times. They defrost quickly and can be added to the tomato sauce with a sautéed onion. The two-minute process to set the meal on its course is: Cut up the onion and slice the sausages into 1-inch pieces. Sauté the onion and sausage in butter or olive oil until the onion is translucent and the sausage is browned. Cover with the tomato sauce and simmer for half an hour. Right before serving, add a generous handful of grated Parmesan, reserving some to sprinkle on top of the pasta. The dish can be served solo, on top of pasta, or, if you have a hungry crew, stuffed in a baguette with melted mozzarella. Dinner—done.

TUNA AND PASTA

The Deans posit that everyone is so crabby today not because of the economy, but because they are not getting enough carbohydrates. Also, need we point out that pasta is cheap, so if we all ate a bit more of it, we would be happy not only because we would finally be satiated, but also because of that peppy jingle of extra change in our pockets.

The Deans call this type of cooking Cans, Jars, Bottles, and Boxes. This recipe is pantry cooking at its finest, taking ten minutes and delivering a meal you could proudly serve to a James Beard Award–winning chef, if one happened to drop by your house around dinnertime. The recipe was procured after a night of reveling at the local nightclub in Monrovia, Liberia. Dean Pollak was with her friends Marco and Franco, two Italian doctors who were among her first culinary instructors. After boogying down everyone needed a carbo load before finally saying good night, so Marco and Franco went into their kitchen pantry and pulled out the ingredients to make this tuna pasta. In Dean Pollak's memory, it still stands head and shoulders above all others. *SERVES 2 TO 3*

½ pound spaghetti

One 7-ounce can oil- or water-packed albacore tuna, drained

1 large bunch fresh flat-leaf parsley, stems discarded and leaves chopped

2 tablespoons unsalted butter, softened

2 to 3 tablespoons heavy cream

1 teaspoon freshly ground black pepper

Pinch of salt

¼ cup finely grated Parmesan

Bring a large pot of salted water to a boil. Add the pasta and cook according to the package directions.

Meanwhile, in a bowl, mash the tuna with a fork. Add the parsley, butter, cream, pepper, and salt and continue to mash with fork until a creamy sauce emerges.

Reserve a few tablespoons of pasta water, then drain the pasta. Add the pasta and the reserved pasta water to the sauce. Toss well. Serve with the Parmesan.

THE OMELET

When you feel that your stamina can withstand only five minutes of cooking, an omelet is in order. Taking out the skillet and melting the butter is half the work. Depending on the ages, appetite, and size of your family members, crack 2 to 3 eggs per person into a bowl and whisk; season with salt and pepper. Melt butter in a skillet over medium-high heat and pour in the eggs. As soon as they are set, cover half of the eggs with your favorite filling (sautéed spinach; chopped cherry tomatoes or any vegetable; shredded cheese; crumbled bacon; diced ham). Fold the other half of the eggs over the filling and slide onto your dinner plate.

PICK-ME-UP MEALS

Sometimes lack of time is not your hurdle. Sadness, loneliness, pity parties: These beset even the jolliest of cooks. At these moments, choose the food that satisfies most.

A ROAST

Dean Manigault's go-to solution for improving her outlook is roasting up chicken or beef. When she sees a standing rib roast on sale, she buys it because serving one always makes her feel like a queen, regardless of her previous mood. (In fact, the aroma of anything roasting improves the spirits of the entire household.) Coat a rib roast with sea salt and lots of black pepper and, if you are feeling zippy, smear it with crushed garlic. Pop it in the oven at 375°F and roast until your meat thermometer, tells you it's done (about 125°F), roughly 17 minutes per pound. Easy, elegant, and uplifting.

CHEESY RICE

Dean Pollak's mood elevator is a dinner of rice. She feels nurtured when she eats a bowlful. When Dean Pollak's husband is away, she soothes herself with a dinner of carbs and fat, dietitians be damned. Bring equal amounts of rice, water, and whole milk to a boil, then simmer for 20 minutes; fold in plenty of grated Parmesan and cracked black pepper. Soul satisfying.

"Prolonged exposure to the same people causes the group to stop exerting effort."

CONVERSATION STARTERS

Menu planning isn't the only aspect of nightly meals that can get stuck in a rut. The dynamics of the eaters can as well. Prolonged exposure to the same people causes the group to stop exerting effort. But going out to a restaurant should not be your only solution to change things up. Instead, invite one or two friends over. This forces the diners to find a topic of mutual interest. The guest's presence is enough to put everyone on their best behavior and a livelier dinner will ensue.

Another way to enliven your mealtime is to have everyone engage in a shared activity. The inventor of Tylenol credits part of his entrepreneurial success to the fact that he is the youngest of seven children and participated nightly in mental gymnastics. Growing up, everyone, regardless of age, had to look up a word, describe it, and use the word in a sentence. Every night seems like too much of a good thing to the Deans, but once or twice a week is definitely diverting.

Mealtime triage is also needed for empty-nest syndrome. Talking to children for eighteen years over dinner is nowhere near as difficult as when they leave and you and your spouse are left face to face alone. The Deans don't know of one couple that has not found the deafening silence of an empty nest daunting. Many couples resort to eating dinner on a tray in front of the TV, and the Deans are not saying they have never done that. However, since we work our butts off in the kitchen and espouse the cooking of great food, we want mindful eating and compliments during the consumption of our creations. There is a reason that frozen TV dinners are so disgusting. No one pays attention while eating them, so it does not matter what is in them. Dinnertime is the time to communicate. No one wants to look back and wonder what happened to all those years while you watched *Law and Order* during dinner. Make one of your primary jobs at home finding a dinner topic more edifying than "Do we need a new washer or can we just fix the old one?"

FRIENDLY OUTREACH

An impromptu invitation to enjoy a family meal can be a godsend to a person feeling down, and their presence can be a godsend to your family dynamic. We know this from firsthand experience. There have been times in the Deans' lives when circumstances laid us low and the reaching out of a kindhearted friend has never been forgotten. A simple meal, even a hot dog or peanut butter sandwich, prepared by someone else, can change a person's outlook. No need to talk about the elephant in the room—the point is to let your friends enjoy a few hours of distraction from an intractable problem.

This can include inviting another mom into the kitchen for moral support—hers *or* yours. Rafts of children can be fed much more easily when there is more than one mother at the helm, even if the two are only drinking wine while they feed the hordes. It's the kind of camaraderie that we all crave at one time or another.

SLOW FOOD

Some recipes need to be on a low flame all day but require very little work. Nothing is more luxurious than a day at home spread out before you with its infinite possibilities as yet untapped. (We give a special caveat to those at home alone with toddlers: A day with them is not leisurely.) When the Deans are gifted with one of these days, we like to turn our attention to slow braising and roasting—one pot on the oven and one pot stovetop. Some flavors and textures refuse to reveal themselves until they are gently teased out with impossibly long cooking times using barely perceptible heat. Thus, our favorite activity (spending hours at home doing very little) coalesces with a feast for supper. If you try this, be sure to go outside and take a brief walk so you can experience entering your house and having an overwhelming olfactory sensation.

BRAISED COLLARDS

The slow cooking of this recipe makes it the ideal accompaniment to the slow-cooked pork below, but these greens are delicious anytime. The braising liquid can be water, white wine, stock, or even leftover Champagne, if you are lucky enough to have any, but the Deans' favorite is chicken stock mixed with beer. We think what makes these leaves over-the-top delicious is the beer-bacon combo.

Wash the collards three times, until all grit is removed. These curly leafed greens only give up their residue of Mother Earth after repeated washings. *SERVES 8 TO 10*

¾ pound thick-cut bacon, diced

3 cups thinly sliced onions

1 large head garlic, minced

4 pounds collards, washed, ribs removed, and leaves chopped

8 cups chicken stock

2 bottles beer

1 ham hock

1 tablespoon Old Bay Seasoning

1 teaspoon sugar

Salt and freshly ground black pepper

Malt vinegar or pepper vinegar, for serving

In a Dutch oven, cook the bacon until crisp. Using a slotted spoon, transfer to a plate.

Add the onions and garlic to the bacon fat and cook until softened. Add the greens and toss once or twice, then add the chicken stock, beer, ham hock, Old Bay, and sugar. Cook over medium-low heat for 2 hours.

Re-crisp the bacon in a skillet until sizzling hot and crisp. Place a colander over a saucepan and drain the greens so the liquid goes into the saucepan. Return the greens to the dutch oven. Off the heat, toss with the bacon; season with salt and pepper. Serve immediately so the bacon does not get soggy, with vinegar on the side.

Use the reserved cooking liquid—what Southerns call pot likker—as a soup the next day. Combine 2 cups pot likker with 1 cup leftover collards (serve with a piece of cornbread).

PORK BUTT IN MILK

The Deans take their toques off to Marcella Hazan. She introduced American cooks to the technique of roasting pork in milk. But her recipe set the Deans to wondering—if a pork loin cooked for two hours in milk was delicious, how much more delicious would a pork butt cooked for six be? We decided to find out firsthand. We expected tasty, but we weren't prepared for our Academy slippers to be blown straight off our feet, which is exactly what happened. *SERVES 8 TO 10*

1 bone-in pork butt
  (about 8 pounds)
½ cup salt

½ cup sugar
Freshly ground black pepper
2 cups whole milk

Place the pork butt fat side up in a roasting pan. Rub the salt and sugar all over the fat. Refrigerate the butt for 1 to 3 hours.

Preheat the oven to 300°F.
Season the butt with pepper. Pour in the milk. Roast in the oven, uncovered, for 6 hours.

CABBAGE SLAW, THE PORK'S PERFECT PARTNER

SERVES 8

½ red cabbage, shredded

6 bunches scallions, chopped

1 large knob of ginger, minced
(use a mini food processor
if you have one), (2 to 3
tablespoons)

2 tablespoons olive oil

2 teaspoons light soy sauce

1 tablespoon rice wine vinegar

Salt and freshly ground black
pepper

In a large bowl, mix all the ingredients and let macerate for up to 1 hour. Make banh mi sandwiches the next day with leftover pork and cabbage; sprinkle with chopped jalapeño.

ICE CREAM SUNDAES TO COMPLEMENT A PORK BUTT DINNER

SERVES 8

CANDIED NUTS

1 egg white

½ pound nuts (hazelnuts, walnuts, pecans, or almonds)

⅓ cup brown sugar

⅓ cup granulated sugar

1 teaspoon cinnamon

½ to 1 teaspoon cayenne

½ teaspoon salt

CARAMEL SAUCE

1½ cups sugar

⅓ cup water

1 cup heavy cream

1 teaspoon pure vanilla extract

SAUTÉED PINEAPPLE OR
BANANAS

2 tablespoons unsalted butter

1 pineapple, skinned, cored, and
sliced, or 4 bananas, halved
lengthwise

2 pints vanilla ice cream

MAKE THE CANDIED NUTS: Preheat the oven to 300°F. In a large bowl, whip the egg white until frothy. Toss in the nuts. Transfer the nuts with a slotted spoon to a bowl with the sugars, cinnamon, cayenne, and salt; toss. Spread the nuts on a parchment-covered baking sheet. Bake for 30 minutes. (The nuts can stored in an airtight tin for up to 1 week.)

MAKE THE CARAMEL SAUCE: In a saucepan, heat the sugar and water over low heat until the sugar is melted. Bring to a boil and cook until medium brown, 5 to 6 minutes. Watch carefully because the mixture can turn black in a moment. Carefully pour in the heavy cream and vanilla extract. Stir over low heat until thickened. Serve warm or at room temperature. (The sauce can be refrigerated in an airtight container for up to 3 days.)

MAKE THE SAUTÉED PINEAPPLE OR BANANAS: In a medium skillet, melt the butter over medium-high heat. Add the pineapple slices or banana halves and cook until caramelized on one side, about 5 minutes. Flip and caramelize the second side. Do not be afraid to get the sides very dark brown—fruit will be even more delicious.

Assemble the sundaes with the ice cream, fruit, caramel sauce, and nuts any way you wish.

GET SOME FRESH AIR

Not only do the Deans hold PhDs in household management, we like to think of ourselves as medical doctors as well. We are convinced that Seasonal Affective Disorder can be cured with more than just light therapy. A bracing 4:00 a.m. turkey shoot will do more to elevate spirits than any sun lamps ever could. If you are more hands-on about procuring the foods for your table, from shooting to catching to growing, or even if you are a vigilant farmers' market shopper walking from stall to stall, you will be spending more time in the daylight and fresh air, which is the best depression reducer around.

DOVE WITH JALAPEÑO AND BACON

As Deans, we know we should be above having teachers' pets, but we cannot help ourselves. We just love doves. Dove breast wrapped in bacon and stuffed with a sliver of jalapeño is a two-bite wonder. Topping these hors d'oeuvres with a demitasse spoonful of red pepper jelly puts them in the category of exceptional. For those of you who don't have access to a dove field, either start sucking up to those who do, or get out your credit card and order wild Scottish Wood Pigeons from a specialty store. Since doves are the sign of peace, why not bookend your meal with two different kinds? Doves for hors d'oeuvres and Dove bars for dessert. What could be more peaceful?

Before wrapping the dove in bacon, the Deans roll the bacon with a rolling pin between two slices of wax paper to make it thinner. We do this because doves are very lean and by the time a regular slice of bacon would be crisp the dove would be overcooked. *SERVES 4*

8 slices bacon, rolled very thin, and halved crosswise, plus 1 regular slice
8 dove or pigeon breasts, (removed from the bone, 16 separate halves)

2 medium jalapeños, seeded and cut into thin slices
2 tablespoons red pepper jelly

Heat a nonstick skillet over medium-high heat. Add the 1 regular slice of bacon and cook until the fat renders, then remove bacon and discard. Place a thin sliver of jalapeño on top of each breast half and wrap with a slice of bacon. Place the wrapped dove breasts in the skillet and fry on one side until the bacon is crisp, then flip and cook the other side, 2 to 3 minutes total. Place the cooked dove breasts on a platter.

Spoon several tablespoons of red pepper jelly into the hot pan to melt, then drizzle over the breasts. Serve immediately with or without toothpicks for skewering. If you have leftovers, let the Deans know if these are good cold. We've never had any.

Why Are We Left Over?
Weren't We Just as Good as
Everyone Else Last Night?

*"The most remarkable thing about my mother is that
for 30 years she served the family nothing but leftovers.
The original meal has never been found."*

CALVIN TRILLIN

Leftovers are a lost art. Everyone's attention is on the recipe of origin and the word *leftover* has become a dirty one. Do you know why there are no leftovers anymore? Two reasons. One, lots of people buy premade, processed food in individual pre-portioned containers. Two, home cooks haven't made a habit of doubling recipes. While roasting one chicken, why not roast a second? A roast chicken may take a little over an hour to cook, but the Deans have a news flash: It takes just as long to roast two or three. You can front-load the work at the beginning of the week or even on the weekend so a meal plan for the week takes shape.

Take chicken. Leftovers from two roast chickens can be made into chicken salad and creamed chicken. Chicken salad and creamed chicken can than be made into an endless variety of dishes: chicken crepes, chicken à la king, or chicken hash. Chicken salad can be made into sandwiches for school lunches or scooped into the cavity of an avocado. What can't leftover chicken do? Being this resourceful will earn you fifteen merit badges, in KP duty.

CREAMY CHICKEN CREPES

Remember how we had you cook two chickens at once? Here's our favorite thing to do with the second one after we've eaten the first. Shred all of the meat from the remaining chicken. If it's holiday time, don't forget that turkey works just as well.

We bet that you have wondered all your life "what is a velouté sauce?" Here it is, ennobling your shredded chicken. *SERVES 4*

CREPE BATTER

2 eggs

1 cup flour

1 cup whole milk

2 tablespoons butter, melted

½ teaspoon salt

CHICKEN MIXTURE

4 tablespoons butter

8 ounces white mushrooms, sliced

¼ cup flour

1½ cups chicken stock

1 cup whole milk

2 cups shredded cooked chicken

1 to 1½ cups grated Parmesan

⅓ cup dry sherry

1 teaspoon salt as needed

MAKE THE CREPE BATTER: Using a standing mixer, or by hand, whisk together all the ingredients. The crepe batter will improve if it sits for 2 hours in the refrigerator, covered with a plate or plastic wrap.

MAKE THE CHICKEN MIXTURE: Preheat the oven to 350°F. In a medium skillet, melt 1 tablespoon butter over medium-high heat until foaming. Add the mushrooms and cook until all the liquid is evaporated.

In a large saucepan, melt the remaining 3 tablespoons of the butter over medium heat until the foaming stops. Whisk in the flour and cook, whisking continuously, until light brown, 2 minutes. Whisk in the stock and milk in a slow stream, reduce the heat to low, and cook, stirring continuously, until the sauce is thick

"It takes just as long to roast two or three."

enough to coat the back of a spoon, about 5 minutes. Add the chicken, mushrooms, and ½ cup Parmesan. Stir in the sherry. Taste for salt and add up to a teaspoon, if necessary.

Make the crepes: In a 7-inch nonstick skillet, melt a tiny bit of butter over medium-high heat until hot but not smoking. Your first crepe will never ever be perfectly cooked, but it's still perfect to eat, so keep a little sugar on hand to have a quick snack. Pour ¼ cup of batter into the pan and start swirling immediately to coat the bottom and sides of the pan. Return to the heat to set the crepe, then flip to cook the other side, about 1 minute total. Repeat with the remaining batter until you have 8 crepes. If your crepe batter is not swirling easily, add a tablespoon of milk at a time until thin enough to coat the pan easily. Crepes can be made a couple of hours ahead of time and stacked on a plate.

(You can freeze any extra crepes for up to 1 month for another use.)

Get out your 9-by-13-inch casserole dish. Starting at one end, put the crepe in the pan, fill with ¼ cup of the chicken mixture and roll up. Repeat until all 8 crepes are filled and nestled together snug in their bed, one against the other. (You can make the crepes to this point and refrigerate them up to 1 day ahead; if you do, add 15 minutes to the baking time.) At this time, the Deans are going for two different end results. Dean Manigault covers her crepes with the remaining chicken sauce and ½ cup of Parmesan, because she likes a creamy, soft consistency. Dean Pollak continues making a few extra crepes to use up all the filling. She is going for a crispy top to contrast the creamy interior. She tops the crepes with 1 cup of Parmesan. Either way, bake the crepes for 30 minutes.

Chicken is not the only food that transforms into marvelous leftovers. A seven- or eight-pound leg of lamb is way too big for most families to eat in one night (lamb used to be a harbinger of spring, but with modern farming practices, lamb is available year-round). Tasty treats can be anticipated all week long. Chops are delicious but a little precious and expensive for family dining. Shoulder is more than good, but not very big. A leg is all things to all people. The original meal is coveted by all, but please don't forget the mint jelly if Dean Manigault is coming over, and if you have invited Dean Pollak, pass the jelly under the table. As for the leftovers, potatoes and lamb are a marriage made in culinary heaven. When you have mashed potatoes, make extra for lamb shepherd's pie a few nights later. If a sandwich is what you crave, try a thick slice of sourdough crisped in hot olive oil, layered with ricotta salata or feta, pitted niçoise olives, roasted peppers, and shaved red onion. Just be sure you thinly slice the lamb, because thick pieces of chilled roasted red meat can be difficult to bite into.

CLEOPATRA'S LAMB SALAD

The lamb itself would happily sacrifice his other three legs if he was prom-ised that their final resting ground would be Cleopatra's favorite Lamb Salad. Dean Pollak is old enough to remember eating this salad with Cleopatra, when she lived in Africa. Ah, those were the days . . . Toasted almonds, white raisins plumped in warm sherry, curled scallions, Persian rice, and fresh apricots if you can find them, or dried. This is the meal Cleopatra served Marc Anthony right before he ravaged her. You will have to wait until Academy Volume II is published to find out what Cleopatra served to Caesar. *SERVES 6*

4 cups shredded cooked lamb
   shoulder
5 tablespoons olive oil
¼ cup toasted sesame seeds

2 tablespoons pomegranate
   molasses (available at
   specialty food stores and
   Middle Eastern markets)

¼ cup dry sherry

1 cup golden raisins

¼ cup honey, preferably
wildflower

¼ cup fresh lemon juice

½ teaspoon sea salt

½ teaspoon freshly ground
black pepper

8 cups cooked basmati rice

¼ cup chopped fresh parsley

2 tablespoons chopped
fresh mint

4 fresh apricots, peeled,
pitted, and sliced into
wedges, or 1 cup finely
sliced dried apricots

1 cup blanched slivered
almonds, toasted

1 cup fresh pomegranate
seeds

1 cup scallion greens, sliced
very thin on an angle and
soaked in ice water

In a large skillet, sauté the lamb in 1 tablespoon olive oil until crisp, about 5 minutes. Transfer to a bowl and toss with the sesame seeds and pomegranate molasses. Keep warm.

In a small saucepan, warm the sherry over low heat. Add the raisins (and dried apricots, if using) and keep over low heat until the sherry has been absorbed. Let cool.

In a large skillet, whisk together the remaining 4 tablespoons olive oil, the honey, lemon juice, salt, and pepper over low heat. Toss in the rice, parsley, and mint.

Divide the rice among six large bowls. Pile the lamb in the center. Top with the remaining ingredients: raisins, apricots, almonds, pomegranate seeds, and scallions. Don't worry if you have leftovers— this salad is just as good cold.

PART II

CONTINUING ED

"Chairs love big booty."

Putting the House to Work for You

DINING ROOM

Your pleasure palace

DINING TABLE

A community outreach center

CHAIRS

A booty catcher and a temporary home for your guests

SIDEBOARD

A serving station as well as a dedicated
party closet containing all the props

CHANDELIER

The mood dictator

LIVING ROOM

A corral in which to house feisty revelers

1. DINING ROOM

"Why don't you ever come in here?"

During the Deans' travels around the globe, we have seen some disused dining rooms, and they are not a happy sight. The architect or planner talked the owner into having a formal, dedicated dining room, but the owner has never come to terms with what to do with it, and the neglect shows. The beauty of a well-used room is more than skin deep. A never used room filled with the finest antiques and silver possesses a dead energy. We would rather dine in a tarpaper shack that's hosted thousands of nightly meals. If you only use your dining room three times a year at most, we doubt very much that those are relaxed, fun events. If a space is never used, your inclination will probably be to get out of it as quickly as possible.

Disabuse yourself of the idea that you need eight people to sit in the dining room. If you are just two, that's fine. Just don't plunk yourselves at the two ends of the table, creating a wide chasm between you. Instead, snuggle up. Put one placemat at the head with the other close by, or sit across from each other so you can play footsie. If you are only four people, seat two people on each side, leaving the two heads empty. Even if it is just your family, light a few candles. And, need we say it? "Abandon all smartphones, ye who enter here." Just as the glow of candlelight is romantic and intimate, the light of a smartphone is eerie and isolating. Now your room has gone from looking like an abandoned room to a room with personality.

CROWN ROAST OF PORK

"I wear a crown to be served in the dining room."

A crown roast of pork is a party treat. It is a roast of pork turned on its end and tied in a circle. In order to form the crown, your butcher needs 15 to 16 rib bones, so obviously this is not a dinner for two.

Trichinosis has not been seen in this country for decades, so Americans should cease fearing undercooked pork. A light rose pink means that the meat is cooked but still juicy and flavorful. And, in fact, the USDA has lowered the safety temperature of cooked to 145°F.

If you have bought little paper crowns to go over the chines, adorn your roast after it emerges from the oven. Fill the center cavity with a stuffing of your choice, or leave it empty. Either way is impressive. *SERVES 8 TO 10*

1 crown roast of pork

Salt and freshly ground black pepper

Generously season the roast with salt and pepper 1 to 2 hours before roasting, leaving the roast at room temperature. Preheat the oven to 425°F. Roast until crisp on the outside and an instant-read thermometer registers 145°F on the inside, 1½ to 1¾ hours. Once you pull the roast from the oven, its temperature will rise to 150°F while it takes its mandatory nap for 10 to 15 minutes.

Parade the crown around the table so everyone can ooh and aah—don't be shy. A crown roast of pork is a rare and stirring sight and not one of your guests will want to miss it.

Slice between the bones, planning on 1 to 2 chops per person, depending on their appetite.

2. DINING TABLE

"We have one thousand and one nights in which to play . . ."

There's a basic arithmetic of the table. If you listen to your dining room table, and you should, it will tell you how many people it can handle. Dean Manigault's table wants eight to ten. Dean Pollak's table wants nine. Her old one preferred six or seven, but a table cannot always get what it wants. The trick is to try to arrange people so the space is intimate and people are as close together as possible. This rarely happens at restaurants, which is a reason why dinner parties at home are more personal than going to a restaurant. Forced intimacy creates a fun atmosphere even if everything else goes awry.

The Deans like uneven numbers for small parties—it's always more entertaining. A few singles liven up any group. Don't doubt the Deans on this. When it comes over the Dean's ticker tape that someone is going out of town, we jump all over the spouse left behind. Not only is this a frequent welcome invitation but it also forces the guest to bring his or her A game to the party. Without the comfort and familiarity of their spouse nearby, people will blossom and engage in a totally different fashion.

DINNER FOR THREE

The Deans love dinners for three: They are the coziest dinners of all. For Dean Pollak it means inviting one person and for Dean Manigault it means inviting two. Dinners for three don't require a large recipe or create much mess, everyone talks to one another so lively banter is assured, and the invite can be issued at the last minute. Don't be surprised if the meal goes on all night, because dinners for three are sometimes the most raucous of all, but no one is trapped into staying any longer than they wish to, including you. It's usually easy to extricate yourself from two people while it may be daunting to rise from a table of eight. Your food choices are limitless: Are you in the mood for the world's best five-minute grilled cheese sandwich and a dessert of ice cream sundaes with cherries on top or for an aspirational cheese soufflé with cherries jubilee to follow? There is no right or wrong, just what you feel like creating.

CHERRIES JUBILEE

Cherries Jubilee is an old-fashioned treat that needs to return to the forefront. The Deans love playing with fire, not to mention that attending a jubilee is so much damn fun.

Depending on what's handy on our bar, we make jubilee with bourbon, cognac, or kirsch. If you are serving bourbon Old-Fashioneds to start, the bourbon Cherries Jubilee is a nice way to round out the evening. Perhaps our favorite pairing is a petite beef filet with a green peppercorn cognac sauce followed by cognac-infused Cherries Jubilee. Pyromaniacs can set fire to both dishes, but caution: Petite filets are going to hog all the limelight during the main course, so choose simple steamed vegetables, such as carrots and spinach, to serve alongside. *SERVES 3 TO 4*

1 pound ripe Bing cherries,
   pitted
½ cup sugar
½ tablespoon lemon zest

Juice of 1 lemon
⅓ cup brandy
Vanilla ice cream, for serving

In a heavy medium-sized skillet, combine the cherries, sugar, lemon zest, and ½ teaspoon lemon juice. Cook over low heat until all the sugar is dissolved, 3 to 5 minutes. Increase the heat and cook for 4 to 6 minutes more to release the juices and develop flavor.

Remove from the heat, add the brandy, and light with a long match! Swirl for 30 seconds or so until the flame burns off. Immediately serve over vanilla ice cream.

DINNER FOR FIVE

We would write about dinner parties for five, but neither of us seem to give them. Our parties always seem to go from three to seven. After four decades of entertaining between us, we have gone back and forth on the whys of this and we cannot figure it out. Three, four, six, seven, but not once five.

DINNER FOR SEVEN

If we are not hosting three people, our favorite number of guests is seven, because seven is the largest number that can sit around one table and hold one communal conversation. Any bigger, and the party usually starts breaking down into smaller groups of separate conversations. Several conversations can be fun, but we love the energy of seven people all talking on one topic and nobody being worried that they are not in on the best conversation at the table.

The Deans love to serve food rarely presented in restaurants for parties of seven. A big roast, such as a leg of lamb, a crown roast of pork, or a whole side of salmon, never fail to impress even the most jaded of party guests. Sometimes we experiment with large one-dish meals such as shepherd's pie, chicken potpie, or paella. These wowers can be so jaw-dropping that they serve double-duty as the main course and the main table decoration. Everyone loves picking at an edible centerpiece, and we doubt that you will have any leftovers.

PAELLA

No one has, or ever will, serve paella for two. Paella is a party food, and maybe the best. There are two essentials to this dish: the correct rice and a tasty broth in which to cook it. The best rice choice, Calasparra bomba rice, is available at Spanish and gourmet markets. The combination of the traditional pan and cooking over an open flame produces a crunchy rice crust on the bottom, the hallmark of a great paella. *SERVES 6 TO 8*

SEAFOOD BROTH

2 whole blue crabs (optional but highly recommended), quartered

1 tablespoon olive oil

24 large (16 to 20) head-on shrimp, peeled and deveined, heads and shells reserved

7 cups rich homemade or boxed chicken stock, plus more as needed

18 mussels, cleaned and debearded

12 littleneck clams, cleaned

1 bunch celery, tender center ribs and leaves chopped

¼ teaspoon crushed saffron

1 medium Spanish onion, chopped

SOFRITO

¼ cup olive oil

2 large firm tomatoes, chopped

7 cloves garlic, roughly grated on a box grater

½ teaspoon smoked paprika (sweet or hot according to preference)

PAELLA

½ cup diced Spanish chorizo

1¾ cups rice, preferably Calasparra bomba

12 littleneck clams, cleaned

18 mussels, cleaned and debearded

4 roasted red peppers, seeded and cut into strips

GARNISH

2 teaspoons olive oil

1 clove garlic, chopped

½ cup frozen peas, thawed

Zest and juice of 1 lemon

Outer ribs from 1 bunch celery

¼ cup coarsely chopped flat-leaf parsley

Sea salt and freshly ground black pepper

MAKE THE SEAFOOD BROTH: In a heavy stockpot, crush the crabs with a meat mallet. Add 1 tablespoon of the olive oil and the shrimp heads and shells (reserve the peeled shrimp); toast over medium heat until the shrimp shells turn pink, 3 to 5 minutes. Add the chicken stock, mussels, clams, and the chopped celery ribs and leaves, and bring to a low rolling boil. Cover and simmer for 5 minutes; remove from the heat. Strain through a colander lined with a double layer of cheesecloth over a bowl. Discard the solids. Stir the saffron into the broth. (Can be made up to the day before dinner party.)

MAKE THE SOFRITO: In a paella pan or large skillet, heat ¼ cup olive oil and the chopped onion over medium heat until the onion is lightly browned. Stir in the tomatoes, garlic, and paprika. Reduce the heat and cook in the center of the pan, stirring to prevent scorching, until a deep, thick, dark red sauce forms, 20 to 30 minutes. Can be made up to the day before party.

ASSEMBLE THE PAELLA: Add the chorizo to the sofrito and cook for 2 minutes. Add the rice and stir over medium heat for 1 to 2 minutes. Spread the rice into an even layer and slowly add 5¼ cups of the seafood broth. If the rice appears too dry, add a little more broth and reduce the heat. The rice requires no further stirring, or a crust will not form. Bring to a boil, then reduce the heat and simmer until the broth appears level with the rice, 7 to 9 minutes.

Your seafood placement determines the final look of the paella. Place the clams into the rice and cook for 5 minutes. Add the mussels and cook for 3 minutes. Add the reserved shrimp and red peppers and cook for 2 minutes. Begin checking the bottom of the rice, and if a crust is not forming, increase the heat slightly to ensure a crisp bottom. Remove the pan from the heat and loosely cover with foil. The residual heat will cook the shrimp through. Some of your guests will enjoy watching you create the paella before their very eyes, but be sure to pay attention to timing and temperatures. They matter greatly in this dish.

MAKE THE GARNISH: In a small skillet, warm the teaspoons olive oil over medium heat and add the garlic. Sauté until the garlic is barely brown. Add the peas and lemon zest; remove from the heat and toss with the lemon juice, celery, and parsley; season with salt and pepper. Scatter over the paella. Bring your masterpiece to the table and prepare to bask in the adulation from all your guests.

LAMB SHOULDER

This recipe is a showstopper. All of a sudden the Deans can think of nothing but lamb shoulder. We've always been leg women, but now our attention is riveted on the shoulder and nothing can divert us. Where has this cut been all our lives? We wake up in the morning thinking shoulder. We go to lunch and look at each other and say, "Shoulder." We open our refrigerator at night to cook dinner and pray we have a shoulder to play with. Once you, too, have caught the shoulder craze, lambs everywhere should start covering their shoulders to protect themselves.

The shoulder requires slow cooking in the oven, following an overnight dry rub. Its leftovers have unlimited potential uses (see Cleopatra's Lamb Salad, page 78). *SERVES 6 TO 8*

1 tablespoon cumin seeds
1 tablespoon coriander seeds
1 whole bone-in lamb shoulder
    (4 to 4½ pounds)
2 tablespoons sea salt
1 tablespoon freshly ground
black pepper

½ teaspoon cayenne
½ teaspoon ground cinnamon
3 heads garlic, cloves separated
    but not peeled
2 tablespoons olive oil

In a small, dry skillet, toast the cumin and coriander over medium heat until fragrant. Let cool, then grind in a spice grinder or with a mortar and pestle.

Score the exterior of the lamb shoulder in a diamond pattern ¼ inch deep. In a small bowl, combine the toasted spices, salt, black pepper, cayenne, and cinnamon; rub into the lamb. Place the lamb on a rack-lined baking sheet and refrigerate uncovered for at least 6 hours and up to 18 hours. Preheat the oven to 500°F.

Place the garlic cloves in the bottom of a Dutch oven. Rub the seasoned lamb with olive oil and place on top of the garlic. Cover the pot and place in the oven; reduce the temperature to 300°F. Roast the lamb until the bone freely wiggles, about 3½ hours. Transfer the lamb to a cutting board or platter and let rest for 15 minutes. Squeeze the garlic from the cloves, mash, and use as a condiment for the lamb.

"Lambs everywhere should start covering their shoulders to protect themselves."

3. CHAIRS

"We love big booty."

One of the Deans' bibles is Winston Churchill's "Dissertation on Dining Room Chairs," written for his wife's benefit. Churchill declares that the perfect chair should provide good support for body and arms, but it should not spread out as if it were a plant. Churchill wrote what the Deans instinctively know: If chairs are too wide, they cannot be pulled close together, and so they'll inhibit maximum socialization. Arms, legs, knees, elbows, all accidentally grazing one another, heighten the electricity during a dinner party. A caterer's standard setup may require a 36-inch width per guest, but that is for the ease and comfort of the servers, not the diners.

Until you want to make a major investment of eight to twelve proper dining room chairs, you can use what you have around the house. Dean Manigault used pillows and Dean Pollak used packing crates around low tables until we were old enough to buy our set of booty catchers. We assure you that the dinner parties we gave then were as much fun as the ones we host today. In fact, Dean Pollak recently put a bench on one side of her dining room table so she can press together as many people as possible, then sip her daiquiri and watch the sparks fly.

While we are talking about chairs, the Deans need to tell you about seating arrangements. Placement is an art form that comes naturally to some, but can be learned by all. First and foremost, you need to tell your guests where to sit. A casual flick of the wrist while saying, "Everyone seat themselves" ensures your dinner party is ruined before it even starts. Guests left to their own devices will *always* arrange themselves in the least inspiring manner. Before the guests arrive, get out a piece of paper and write a list of all the men's names in one column and the women's names in another. Draw a diagram of your table and seating spots, designating one line for each guest. Now fill in the lines. The host or hosts sit at the heads. The right side of the host or hostess should be filled by the most honored guest of the opposite sex. Most honored can include: first-time visitors to your house or someone visiting from out of town, the eldest invitee, the highest in stature (i.e., the mayor, the principal, or the dean of the Academy). His or her partner, whether married or cohabitating, sits on the right of your spouse. If you have no spouse, you have an extra hot spot with which to play. Fill the rest of the seats boy-girl-boy-girl, trying to create peppery dynamics. Picture in your mind the conversations happening, or not, as the case may be. Let intuition be your guide. Mix old with young, married with singles, liberals with conservatives. When every one of your guests is a returnee, be sure you don't repeat who sits next to you; otherwise you run the risk of people thinking you are playing favorites. On a final note, if you have an extra guest or two of the same sex, the female goes by the hostess and conversely the male guest goes by the host. You may have to redo your diagram several times, but looking at it will let you know when the seating is ideal.

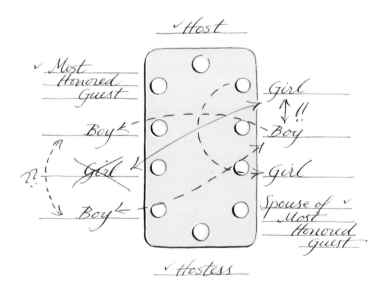

"Now that you know the rules, do as you wish."

4. SIDEBOARD

"We are wallflowers and proud of it."

Sideboards stand at the ready, off to the side and against the wall, in perpetuity. As soon as this wallflower is purchased, you can almost hear your heirs start to squabble over who gets to inherit it. Sideboards are good-looking, functional, stately—and every inch of them is useful. No matter where you dwell, you need more storage space and a sideboard is a most elegant repository for your china and cutlery.

Not everyone has a sideboard, but that does not mean you cannot fashion a temporary buffet table. Other pieces can be shanghaied to serve active duty. A side table from your living room or bedroom can become a station for displaying an array of desserts or appetizers. Just be sure to kennel up any long-legged dogs with frisky tails or the table will be cleared before you want it to be. A sideboard possesses a mystical aura fit for Bacchanalia when the surface is strewn with lush vegetation and an overabundance of candles, dishes, and platters of food.

SHRIMP CURRY

When the Deans used to eat curry on the edges of the Sahara desert, we unfurled carpets on the sand, scattered pillows, and laid out our feast on the ground. These days, we are unable to get to the Sahara as often as we would like, but that does not mean we don't enjoy a spicy curry feast once in a while. We still have our pillows; we just put them around the coffee table and light our braziers. After several puffs on the communal hookah, no one remembers they aren't in North Africa anymore.

Out of our waters we ceaselessly haul the briniest, tenderest crustaceans pulled from any oceans. The most fun part of serving curry is the chance for everyone to play with all the condiments, and when you are lucky enough to show up for curry night at the Academy, you will be stupefied by the dizzying array on offer.

Toasted peanuts or cashews, sliced mango, toasted unsweetened coconut, chopped scallions, chives, fried shallots, plantain chips, edible flowers, and of course chutney (see page 181): These players add the crunch, texture, and color to your curry party. You can pump up the spice on the curry because the condiments help cool and refresh as well. The little bowls of condiments orbit around the central curry dish like mini satellites and create a stunning tablescape for your sideboard. *SERVES 6 TO 8*

5 tablespoons butter

1 small red or yellow habanero chile, seeded and very finely chopped, or 1 jalapeño if you are not feeling brave

1 small onion, chopped

2 tablespoons flour

1 tablespoon curry powder

1 teaspoon sea salt

¼ teaspoon hot smoked paprika

¼ teaspoon ground nutmeg

1 cup shrimp stock (simmer shrimp shells in water for 20 minutes) or chicken stock

1 cup coconut milk

¼ cup finely chopped candied ginger

1 lemon Juice

1 tablespoon dry sherry

Dash of Worcestershire sauce

2½ pounds peeled and deveined shrimp

Cooked rice, for serving

Melt the butter in a large saucepan. Add the chile and onion and sauté over medium-high heat until softened, about 5 minutes. Stir in the flour and cook for 2 to 3 minutes. Stir in the curry powder, salt, paprika, and nutmeg until smooth, and cook for 2 minutes more. Pour in the stock and coconut milk and cook until thickened. Add the ginger, lemon juice, sherry, and Worcestershire sauce.

Add the shrimp and cook until opaque, about 3 minutes. Serve over rice.

"We are unable to get to the Sahara as often as we would like."

5. CHANDELIER

"Turn me down so I can turn you on."

— ◦ —

Tommy Bennett, a scion of one of Charleston's original families, put it best when he said about aging, "The less we can see, the less we should be able to see." Dimmers are essential on every light source in the house, but nowhere more important than on your chandelier. If you are going to use a chandelier in the dining room, turn it to its lowest setting and augment with candles. A chandelier must be hung precisely in the center of the room, no matter what. When it hangs over a table, the bottom of the chandelier should be no more than 30 inches from the surface of the tabletop. Any higher is a travesty.

— ◦ —

OYSTERS ROCKEFELLER

It should come as no surprise that Oysters Rockefeller's closest cousin is a chandelier. They are both retro and they are both mood enhancers. We expect all of you to be serving these briny bivalves under your chandeliers.

Joshua Shea, food and beverage director for Charleston's baseball stadium, won first place for these Oysters Rockefeller in the Charleston Restaurant Association Taste of Charleston competition. We hadn't seen Oysters Rockefeller on menus for years, and the Deans have been wondering where they went. We are thrilled to have been reacquainted with this luxurious presentation of our favorite mollusk. *SERVES 4 AS A FIRST COURSE*

3 tablespoons finely chopped fresh spinach	3 tablespoons chopped scallions
3 tablespoons finely chopped fresh watercress	3 tablespoons chopped fresh parsley
6 tablespoons butter	Salt and freshly ground black pepper
1 tablespoon Pernod	Rock salt

16 oysters, shucked and on
the half shell
Hollandaise Sauce
(recipe follows)

Toasted Bread Crumbs
(see next page)

In a small saucepan of boiling water, blanch the spinach and watercress for 1 minute. Drain, squeeze out any water, and mince. Melt the butter in a medium saucepan. Add the spinach and watercress and cook, stirring continuously, for 1 minute. Add the Pernod and ignite. Once the flame burns out, add the scallions and parsley and cook for 2 minute more; season with salt and pepper. Spread out evenly on a plate, and refrigerate until cold.

Turn the broiler on. Set the rack to the lower third of the oven. Cover a baking sheet with rock salt and nestle the oysters in the salt. Spoon the spinach mixture on top, dividing evenly among the 16 oysters. Top the oysters with 1 heaping teaspoon each of hollandaise and bread crumbs and broil for 10 minutes.

Never take your eye off anything you are broiling. Keep the door ajar and your eye on the prize. If the tops start to darken ominously, remove pan immediately.

HOLLANDAISE SAUCE

Dean Manigault's hollandaise trick is to use a whole stick of cold butter, because the cold from the butter keeps the egg yolks from setting. She plunges her balloon whisk into the side of the stick of butter, and immerses it in the egg yolk mixture. Then she uses her double boiler set over simmering water and, whisks until the butter melts and the hollandaise just sets. *MAKES 1 CUP*

3 egg yolks
Juice of 1 lemon

1 stick (4 ounces) unsalted
butter, chilled
Pinch of salt

In a double boiler over barely simmering water (the water should not touch the bottom of the pan), whisk together the egg yolks and lemon juice until the mixture is thickened, about 5 minutes. Add the whole chilled stick of butter and whisk it in until melted and incorporated and the sauce is thickened and doubled in volume, about 5 minutes more. Remove from the heat and whisk in the salt. Cover and place in a warm spot until ready to use. If the sauce gets too thick, whisk in a few drops of warm water before serving.

TOASTED BREAD CRUMBS

MAKES 1 CUP

4 tablespoons butter
1 cup panko bread crumbs
¼ cup chopped fresh parsley

In a medium skillet, melt the butter. Stir in the panko and parsley and mix thoroughly.

THE BIG BOY

When you are feeling virile and hardy, the time has come to tackle . . . a large dinner party.

We can't fool you—if your party has grown to ten or more people, you have work ahead of you. The physics of entertaining asserts that ten people for dinner is more than twice the work of five. Sixteen people are exponentially more than eight, and so on.

You have to first visualize this event in order to pull it off. Who is coming? Where are these people going to sit? What are their drinks going to be served in, their food on, and which utensils will be used, and how many of them? Right now you are probably thinking, "I will never do this." Incorrect! You will, and you will like it, but the event requires thought and preparation.

Chip away at the jobs over several days, but the days do not have to be consecutive. This is the purpose of your freezer. Some foods can be frozen for up to a month, and in fact, they taste better for it. We want you to think big, but we also want you to be ready. How are you going to break down the shopping, cooking, and table setting into manageable pieces? Liquor shopping fortuitously can be done months ahead—just don't nip at the bottles too often before party day, or you'll have to shop again. With the food cooked and the liquor purchased, you are halfway home.

Gumbo (page 116), meatballs (page 164), cassoulets—all of these are good dishes to put together a month in advance and nestle in your freezer until party time. Just as with childbirth, the labor will be forgotten over time.

If you have gone to all the expense and trouble to make a sumptuous, labor-intensive meal, do not be shy about tooting your own horn a bit at the time of presentation. A quick, "This is not cans of baked beans with weenies thrown in. It is a cassoulet from southwestern France, which has lamb, pork, duck, and European sausages, and it takes two days to assemble. Please enjoy eating it as much as I did making it!" will put every guest in a properly reverential state of mind.

Tables can be arranged and set a few days before, if you have the room; if you don't, do it the night before. If your guest list outstrips your table size, rent a 48-inch round table to seat up to seven extra guests.

A big party is all about creating lists, and really, is there anything more satisfying than checking things off a to-do list? The weight of the world starts slipping from your shoulders with each task that gets a line drawn through it. You are executing a major event that people will remember and that you will feel proud of having accomplished.

The Deans' reasons for hosting large parties currently boil down to two: We either see a large recipe we are compelled to make, or we meet several people we yearn to know better. As young brides we started hosting "big boys" because our china screamed to get out of the cupboard and demanded to be shown off, but as we grew older we came to love the experience and the shared camaraderie that only big dinner parties can offer.

THE LUNCHEON

The Deans feel that a ladies' lunch is an occasion that needs some modernizing. The ladies who lunch today are totally different animals from their grandmothers.

Traditionally, the occasion included an intensive three-course gutbuster—no friend to one's liver. After the meal, bridge was often played or the ladies were driven home to rest.

The Deans have no time to rest and you don't either. More often than not, our lunch guests are business associates and our dining room becomes a boardroom. The Deans make every second count by serving a one-course man-size salad with man-size croutons.

WHAT TO SERVE AT YOUR PARTY

When it comes to information about food, the Deans realize that there can be too much of a good thing. We can download recipes from every country, we're expected to keep up with the latest food fetish, we're instructed to buy locally, stay heart-healthy, and so on—why, even the Deans get a big fat headache thinking about at all. Stressing about menu choices for a dinner party is not productive. The Deans have a trick to put up your sleeve: You only need to know how to cook one or two things—you just need to cook them better than anyone else does.

"The chicken begins its journey to table with a two-hour bath."

Step one is choosing the basic recipe that never goes out of style. It can be altered later, but for now, the original recipe itself must be top-notch. With a bit of research you can connect the food you most like to the award-winning chef whose recipe appeals to you. For example, we like Jean-Georges Vongerichten's roast chicken recipe above all others. Naturally, the Deans adopted his recipe as our own. The care Jean-Georges lavishes on a simple bird goes a long way to explain why he is known as one of the world's best chefs. His chicken, always of the highest quality, begins its journey to the table by taking a two-hour bath in a wet salt-sugar brine, and is stuffed with lavish amounts of butter and subsequently sautéed in even more butter on top of the stove. Finally, the chicken is roasted and basted in a very hot oven. The Deans are mesmerized by Jean-Georges's way with poultry, because not only is his recipe doable, but it is world-class delicious. We cook it several times a month. We don't waste our time, energy, or money on so-so recipes. Conceivably, you might be serving your selection for the next forty years, so the time spent hunting for a top-notch dish is well worth it. (Needless to say, every recipe in this book was researched so thoroughly on the front end that they have been pleasing us for decades.)

The only way to achieve perfection is through practice. Don't try a recipe for the first time when people are coming over. The dish prepared the second or third time is always faster to make and tastier. After five times you've got it down to a science and won't be hovering over the stove; you will be multitasking. When to practice? With everyday cooking for your family, of course!

The Deans feel strongly that a three-course meal is plenty, and two courses are often enough. Guests can feel trapped at the table and wonder if they mistakenly signed up for a Chinese banquet if the courses keep coming.

AVOID MENU ANGST

If a host has to worry about your dietary restrictions on top of the setting and seating of the table, the music and ideal mood lighting, etc., then home entertaining will cease to exist. The onus of satisfying a myriad of food restrictions makes entertaining too difficult for the art form to sustain.

An invitation to dinner in someone's house is a gift that is not equal to meeting at a restaurant. Your meal choices end when you accept the invitation. Unless your allergy is life threatening, there's no need to detail every aspect of what you will or will not eat for whatever reason. Bring your best attitude and eat what you can.

Hosts must relax as well. There are many reasons why a guest might not eat everything on his plate and it's not up to the host to discover why. If we expect guests to be quiet about what they cannot eat, then hosts need not ask about what guests leave behind.

Let us not lose the real point of home entertaining: giving guests an intimate view of yourself by letting them see how you live. Entertaining should not be fraught with worries over gluten. Once your guests arrive, assign food a secondary role and focus on the sharing of our homes and all the other ingredients that go into building and celebrating relationships.

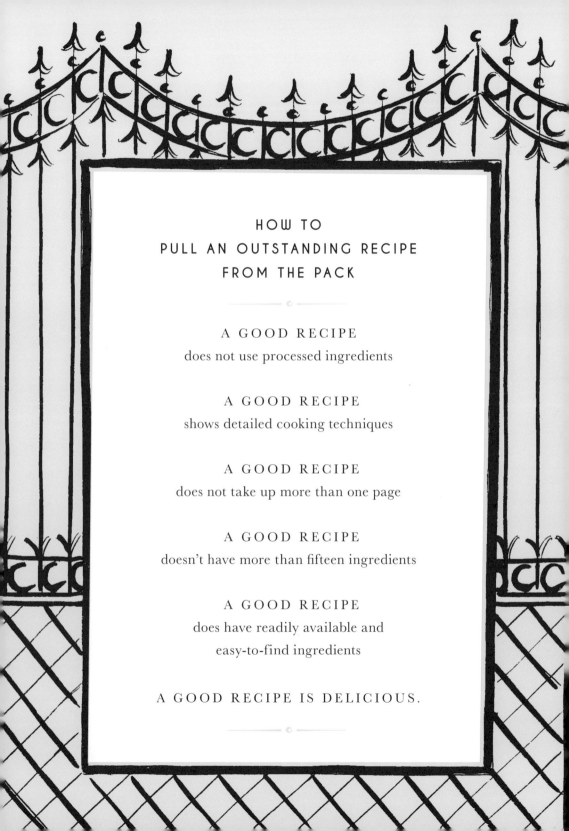

HOW TO
PULL AN OUTSTANDING RECIPE
FROM THE PACK

A GOOD RECIPE
does not use processed ingredients

A GOOD RECIPE
shows detailed cooking techniques

A GOOD RECIPE
does not take up more than one page

A GOOD RECIPE
doesn't have more than fifteen ingredients

A GOOD RECIPE
does have readily available and
easy-to-find ingredients

A GOOD RECIPE IS DELICIOUS.

THE GUEST LIST—MIXOLOGY

Making a guest list is akin to making a cocktail. The blending and contrast of ingredients (or guests) determines the final outcome of the festivity. When deciding whom to invite it is important to think about getting some sex in the room. Sex appeal is necessary for the energy of a party and always has been. The energy of two people sparking a friendship permeates the room and is even better when more than two people find one another. Your guests feel like something is happening, this is an event, I'm glad I'm here, and tonight is going to be more exciting than usual. Start sexing up your party by inviting someone *you* want to get to know better.

Dean Manigault has a posse and she likes a lot of them to be in attendance at every event she holds. Without a port in the storm, walking into a room of strangers makes her acutely uncomfortable. She looks for a familiar face so she can anchor herself for the evening. A conversation with someone she knows relaxes her.

Dean Pollak is thoroughly energized by "The Shock of the New." She truly embraces the adage that a stranger is a friend she hasn't met yet. She doesn't know how someone might change her life, but she lives with the expectation that one of the unknowns will.

The Deans insist there should be some cohesion to the guest list, but not too much. The point is to mix ages, sexes, professions, interests, couples, singles, nationalities. A group of one kind of people is stale. Let your house be known as the one where the best parties are held because the guests can never be sure whom they are going to meet.

Not everyone you have invited to your party has the same strengths. You'll have some talkers, some thinkers, some non-talkers and some non-thinkers and of course, everyone's favorite, the non-thinking talker. But whatever. For one night, they are all together and it's your job to see that they get along. Let guests know the most salient facts about the other invitees. How is Suzanne to know that Lee is an expert on raising guinea hens unless you tell her? By pointing out common interests between your various party animals, you get the energy flowing in the right direction.

"The energy of two people sparking a friendship permeates the room."

The moment your guest walks in your house is the most important moment of the evening. Your enthusiasm sets the stage: Every single person who walks in your door should feel like the star of the evening. This includes the dud spouse of your best friend and the relative who drives you the most crazy. Simply by your being fascinated by them, the guests begin to *feel* fascinating, and others wonder what you are seeing that they don't. Here is the trick: Tonight you are not pretending. You *believe* everyone in your house is a star and should be treated accordingly. A party of supernovas never fails.

There are some sad truths in the world and the saddest may be that not everyone is going to want to come to your party. There may be no reason, or the reasons may be limitless, but the fact is, once you have had two or three rejections from the same person, move on. There are plenty of people who are dying to come to your parties, so focus on them and do not speculate about why someone said no. You will never guess correctly.

If a guest texts or calls the host on the day of the event to cancel (unless it's a true emergency), there is a troubling lack of respect. Money and effort have already been spent on his behalf. Abusing a host with such a last-minute brush-off guarantees that the invited won't be invited again. Just as bad is a noncommittal response. "I'll try" or "Maybe" are meaningless platitudes that tell hosts nothing about the number of guests we can expect. We would rather hear "no" than "maybe." The Deans have spoken to countless party givers, and have experienced themselves these rejections and the ensuing havoc. It's not that the guests themselves are irreplaceable treasures, it's that there is no time left in which to replace them. The last-minute cancellation says in the baldest way that you have found something better to do and have chosen to do that instead. Ouch! Our final instruction: Do not let your invitations age like a fine wine hoping you will get a better one. We know what you are up to. When you receive an invitation, you have one to two days in which to respond, unless the invitation is via text or phone, in which case your response should be immediate. An immediate no is more welcome than a yes that transforms into a no later.

Thanking people is a cinch. But the Deans have noticed a new trend that we can't like. People bring a hostess gift in lieu of thanking us later. To this trend, we say "no thank you." Save your money, and instead lavish us with your praise and post-party wrap-up. We want the breakdown of our party: What did you think, who did you like, who did you not like, what did you talk about, did you go out afterward. From our delicious buffet, which dish did you enjoy most? Did you drink too much, not enough? To all these questions and more, we want answers. A handwritten note, a phone call, a detailed text, or an e-mail are all acceptable. Silence is not.

WHAT TO WEAR . . .

The Deans have thought long and hard about how we dress. We have principles about what to wear at our house, your house, a restaurant. Let us share.

Being overdressed is as bad as being underdressed. Sometimes worse. Jackie Onassis did not get the title "Best-Dressed Woman in the World" by running around in formal wear twenty-four hours a day. She always dressed appropriately for the occasion at hand. The Deans have seen people dress in black tie for a five o'clock event because the venue was palatial. Unless you are attending the Oscars and it's being broadcast for the East Coast, it's not okay to go that fancy for something that early. If the start time is before 7:30 p.m., the event is *not* black tie.

. . . AT OUR HOUSE

When we entertain at our house, we have to be comfortable, so we always take off our shoes. The informality of this gesture immediately puts others at ease. The fancier our clothes, the more likely we are to shed our shoes early, if we bother to put them on at all. Remember, we only do this at our own houses. We promise we will not be trotting around barefoot in yours.

As for our hair, we simply cannot have it flying around and landing in our delicious food. Disgusting. Hair of the home cook must be held back.

Grease will inevitably find a way to attach itself to dangling bracelets and low-hanging necklaces while you finish last-minute cooking—remove. Rings are magnets for dough and uncooked meat—remove. Having eliminated all other jewelry choices, the Deans rely on big earrings for parties (they do not have to be real gemstones, just eye-catchers).

Watch out for long or batwing sleeves. They not only gather food, even worse, they might ignite and set the hostess on fire. Please let common sense always be your guide.

. . . AT YOUR HOUSE

When we're invited to your house for dinner, the first thing we'll think about is our shoes. This is the moment to put on our most beautiful pair. While we sit in your living room sipping a cocktail, our shoes are enjoying their time in the spotlight. They are not hidden under a table, as they would be in a restaurant. And let's face it; at least among women, shoes are a great conversation starter. They have the ability to get half the room onto common ground. But remember, your shoes are your pedestal. If your feet hurt before you get in the car to leave your house, you are going to hate your shoes within the next forty-five minutes, no matter what they look like. Your sparkling wit and sunny personality cannot be in evidence when your feet are killing you.

"The Deans rely on big earrings."

. . . AT A RESTAURANT

When getting dressed to go to a restaurant, your first step is to assess your strengths. The focus is on your waist up, because the rest of you is hidden under the table. What are your primary assets: cleavage, neck, arms, hair? If it's all of these, you don't need the Deans' advice. Otherwise, pick one or two body parts and showcase them. A glittering comb in the hair, a sleeveless dress, a low-buttoned silk top, you get the picture. No need for teetering high heels, because no one can see your shoes anyway.

6. LIVING ROOM

Every domicile has a living area, ipso facto, everyone can host a great cocktail party. If you have a dedicated living room there is a good chance that you never go into it. Why has all the fun been moved to the kitchen and family rooms? People tend to put their best furniture and artwork in their living rooms and then close the door on this room forever. The Deans want you to throw the door wide open, inhale deeply, and plunge forward into your new life together. The single best use for a living room is a jolly jump-up. Make your living room your party room.

AT-HOME GETAWAYS: IT'S TIME FOR BRUNCH

Daytime parties are inherently more relaxing than evening events. Lounging around sets the mood of these gatherings, so if you have a pool, an outdoor or indoor fireplace, or a garden with seating, use these spaces. For maximum frivolity, urge your energetic guests to participate in a shared activity, while the more sedate among you cheer them on. Crossword puzzles, swimming, bocce ball, ping-pong, badminton, or volleyball—an activity adds to the enjoyment of every guest. (Having your guests do all the dishes does not count as a pleasurable shared activity.)

Daytime parties like these are rare and welcome. The benefits are: less expense (only those held most firmly under the sway of the demon drink will overimbibe midday), fewer courses to serve (two are more than sufficient), and your house can be put back together by bedtime.

The meal that suits the daytime party best is Saturday lunch or Sunday brunch. The Deans debated the whys, wheres, and whens of brunch and one point became evident: Brunch is an exclusively Sunday affair. If you have a midday gathering on Saturday, it's a luncheon. The Saturday lunch/ Sunday brunch divide, unwritten about until now, transcends continents and generations. We have been to Saturday lunches and Sunday brunches in places from Newport to Mogadishu. Another clear point: The start time for both parties is one o'clock.

A brunch needs an anchor and out-of-town guests can be ideal ones. They have unstructured time they are looking to fill. A brunch lets them see inside a local's house, then leaves them open to try the hot spots for dinner.

Another excuse to brunch you may not have thought of: Invite the guests from the night before back over for brunch the following day. In other words, if you've put together an eclectic group, consider giving them two invitations at once, one for dinner and one for brunch the next day. This sounds crazy, and it is, a little, but it is an incredibly fun thing to try, and the one-two punch means that your events will never be forgotten. This combo plan is a way of creating forced intimacy in an eighteen-hour period. The key is to make sure that the guests are not each other's best friends because the unknown dynamic is what creates the electricity.

There are some crossover foods and drinks that are acceptable to serve both Saturday and Sunday, but some things are only for brunch. A crossover drink is a Bloody Mary, but mimosas are strictly Sunday sippers. (Could this mean mimosas are divine?) For Saturday a quiche is a no-brainer, but other egg-centric dishes such as scrambled eggs, eggs benedict, or egg stratas are sacred to Sunday. If you go the breakfast route, you can choose to be a short-order cook flipping pancakes or frying eggs, or you could have made an egg casserole several days ahead and put it in the oven that morning. Starting lunch at one o'clock means you have enough time to get prepared, and your guests, do too. And one o'clock frees up the types of food you can serve, so don't feel limited to serving just eggs and bacon. Some of our favorite selections are interactive foods: fried chicken because it can be eaten with your hands, a fully laden curry feast with all its attendant condiments, or how about Oysters Rockefeller and Champagne?

HOW TO INHERIT
YOUR GRANDMOTHER'S SILVER:

A Primer

The Deans are big advocates for inheriting, whether the inheritance is in the form of a sterling silver set for twenty-four or the searing insights that your grandmother learned through the course of her life. Right now is the last time in history that the permanently plugged-in will have access to a family member who grew up using a party line.

If you really feel that you are the rightful heir to your family's treasures, then it's never too early to start jockeying for position. Ten years old, however, is the absolute oldest that you can get away with asking point-blank, "Can I inherit the silver?" So, for all you ten-and-unders, ask away. If, however, you have missed this crucial deadline, hope is not lost. By showing interest and asking your grandmother and her friends about the important stories behind the objects, you demonstrate that you are worthy of being the custodian of these valuable links to the past. And along with the honor of inheriting the silver, you have also inherited the duty to pass along the stories to future generations.

If you are going to all this trouble to inherit, collect, beg, borrow, or steal table settings, then you better use them. Objects from the past are itching to be used. Nothing infuriates the Deans more than walking into a museum of a house with a beautifully laid dining room table set with eighteenth-century silver and china for a party that will never be. Too depressing. You might as well drape clear vinyl over your best upholstery. There is no point in showing off your interior if that is simply all you are doing—showing off. It also sickens the Deans to hear that your finery is sitting in a dusty closet while you are perpetually eating food from a container. This is not living; this is waiting to live. Ridiculous! Even if the evening meal is Chinese takeout, eat the food off

"There was a specific utensil for every imaginable purpose."

of a proper plate and use the correct utensils. We guarantee dinner will taste better and you will feel more gracious.

The reason to use your silver is not to preen; it's to subtly improve the quality of your life. So, start polishing. The Deans are going to teach you that everyday living is more important than the grand occasion. A bit of extra effort spent every day adds up to a life well lived. Don't you love your family way more than that mysterious potentate who may never be coming anyway?

The good news is that gracious living is not that difficult to achieve. We are not in the Victorian age when the table was set with a hundred different objects. In that era, there was a specific utensil for every imaginable purpose (petit-four forks, orange knives, strawberry spoons, among other arcane pieces). However, these esoteric items can be fun to collect and repurpose for imaginative new uses.

The rules of setting the table exist for the same purpose as any other etiquette rules—to make people feel comfortable. The only rule you must know about place settings is to work from the outside in and worry about the stuff on top later: Forks go on the left on top of the napkin; knives go on the right (knife blades facing to the left); and spoons go to the right of knives.

The setting for dessert is where the Deans bid each other adieu. Dean Manigault places her dessert fork to the right of her dinner fork and her dessert spoon to the left of the dinner knife. This puzzles Dean Pollak to no end as she has always placed her dessert fork and spoon above the dinner plate.

As for the dishes . . . Water glasses go on the top-right of the plate and wine glasses to the left of the water glass. Butter plates, if using, go to the left of the dinner plate, as do the salad plates, if serving a salad with the main meal instead of as a separate course. If using both butter and salad plates, the butter plate sits above the salad plate. We feel this is too many plates to crowd on one table, so the Deans never use butter plates and we think salad deserves a course of its own, but if you like this idea, this is the correct placement.

Of course, you will need to first lay your base. A beautiful tablecloth is a wonderful thing but caring for it is not. It's time- and labor-intensive to clean, and therefore the Deans more frequently use placemats. The placemats the Deans find the most useful are plain laminated wood trimmed in gold leaf, with felt undersides. They are an expensive initial outlay but they last forever, can be dressed up or down, are easily cleaned, and, with proper care, can be inherited by your grandchildren along with your grandmother's silver.

ONE-OF-A-KIND PIECES

LARGE TABLESPOON The main reason Dean Pollak loves gumbo so much is that it allows her to use the large silver spoons her good friend Father Ralston gave her and, by doing so, remember him. She serves the delicious dish over Thanksgiving weekend, which is Dean Pollak's favorite holiday. The Sunday after Thanksgiving, she starts strategizing for next year's holiday. A trick she can put up your sleeve is to start making gumbo a month before Thanksgiving. With the gumbo waiting in the freezer and the silver polished, you have a stress-free party ready to go weeks ahead of time.

GUMBO

SERVES 8

⅓ cup vegetable oil

⅓ cup flour

1 whole chicken

1 large yellow onion, quartered

1 cup diced celery, plus chopped
    leafy tops from 1 bunch celery

1 bay leaf

2 tablespoons coarse salt

¼ cup olive oil

1 cup diced green bell pepper

1 cup diced red onion

1 teaspoon crushed red pepper

½ teaspoon freshly ground white
    pepper

½ teaspoon freshly ground black
    pepper

¾ teaspoon gumbo filé

¾ teaspoon dried thyme

6 cloves garlic, finely chopped

½ pound bacon, coarsely
    chopped

1 pound smoked andouille
    sausage, cut into ¼-inch-thick
    slices

One 16-ounce can tomato puree

1 pound large shrimp, peeled
    and deveined (optional)

Cooked rice and cornbread, for
    serving

Place the vegetable oil and flour in a small saucepan and whisk over medium heat to combine. Cook, whisking constantly, until the mixture turns a very dark color, 12 to 15 minutes. Transfer this roux to a small bowl and let cool to room temperature, then drain the excess oil. (The roux can be made ahead and refrigerated for 24 hours.)

Place the chicken, yellow onion, celery tops, and bay leaf into a large stockpot and add water to cover. Add the salt, and bring to a boil over medium-high heat. Lower the heat and simmer until the chicken is tender and the water is infused with flavor, about 1 hour. Transfer the chicken to a plate and let cool. Strain the stock into a large measuring cup and reserve (if needed, stir in enough water to make 4½ cups). When the chicken is cool enough to handle, strip the meat from the bones and shred it into large pieces. Wipe out the stockpot and reserve.

In a large saucepan, warm the olive oil over medium-high heat. Add the green pepper, diced celery, and red onion. Cook, stirring occasionally, until the vegetables begin to soften and color slightly, 12 to 15 minutes.

In a small bowl, combine the red pepper, white and black peppers, filé, and thyme; sprinkle over the vegetable mixture. Cook, stirring continuously, for 8 minutes. Mix in the garlic and cook for 3 minutes more.

In a large saucepan, heat the reserved stock over medium heat. Place the roux in the stockpot in which you cooked the chicken. Whisk ¼ cup of the warm stock into the roux until it forms a smooth paste. Add the remaining stock, along with the vegetables, stirring well to combine. Bring the mixture to a boil, reduce the heat, and simmer for 1 hour.

Meanwhile, in a heavy skillet, cook the bacon until crisp. Remove the bacon and add the sausage to the same skillet. Cook for a few minutes.

Add the tomato puree, crisped bacon and sausage to the stockpot. Simmer until the gumbo is thick, about 30 minutes. Add the chicken. (The gumbo can be made ahead to this point and refrigerated for up to 2 days or frozen for up to 3 weeks.)

Stir in the shrimp, if using, and cook until pink, about 15 minutes. Serve over rice with cornbread.

GRAPEFRUIT SPOONS   Tit on a boar hog? Wrong! You've just been thinking about them incorrectly. The Deans pine in vain for the day when eight strong sat at a table and expected that breakfast would be served by Jeeves. Although this is not likely to happen anytime soon, you can still use the sharp little spoons of that bygone era. By taking a grapefruit and running it under the broiler to caramelize the sugar, you can create an elegant, easy, and salubrious dessert, the Deans' favorite kind. This dessert saves those grapefruit spoons from a lifetime of obscurity. Another trick: If you do not own eight spoons, and have just one, don't despair! The saw-edged teeth around the tip of the spoon can be employed in the use of removing seeds from cucumbers.

ICED TEA SPOONS These are highly collectible and can be found in most antique shops. The Deans use the spoons for their intended purpose from midmorning through midafternoon, but by night, we repurpose them for an altogether different excitement: scooping up mouthfuls of elegant desserts. They are simply too beautiful to be relegated to a life in the drawer, so we've thought long and hard about different ways to use them.

PEPPERMINT ICE CREAM SUNDAES

Peppermint ice cream sundaes are Dean Manigault's all-time favorite dessert. They are easy to make; they are soft and smooth; they have a hot-cold contrast, with crunchy bits within. Dean Manigault presents them in her grandmother's parfait glasses, with her iced tea spoons. Her secret is crushed peppermint candies mixed with high-quality vanilla ice cream, such as Häagen-Dazs, and a homemade chocolate sauce. Ladle the hot sauce over two scoops of ice cream for that sundae feeling, whipped cream optional.

CHOCOLATE SAUCE

MAKES 1 CUP

Two 3.5-ounce best-quality dark chocolate bars (70% cacao)
3 tablespoons butter
⅓ cup heavy cream

Melt the chocolate in a double boiler. Swirl in the butter and heavy cream until incorporated and serve immediately over ice cream.

FISH SLICE Dean Pollak uses her fish slice for serving poached whole fish. Dean Manigault finds her fish slice is perfect as a spanking tool.

STUFFING SPOON Dean Manigault is an ardent fan of wet juicy dressing. She uses her stuffing spoon with relish as she excavates the cavity of her turkeys and chickens.

Dean Pollak could not disagree more, and that's why she never goes to Dean Manigault's for Thanksgiving. She plans her own feast, and feels very strongly that her stuffing is best. She prefers crisp stuffing that has never seen the inside of a fowl and is oven-baked in a pan, exposed to the heat. If Dean Manigault would ever come over, she would be a convert. But she won't— that's how firmly the line has been drawn in the sand.

SAUSAGE-MUSHROOM STUFFING

SERVES 8

2 tablespoons butter

1 pound ground pork sausage

1½ onions, finely chopped

2 ribs celery, peeled and thinly
    sliced

2 cloves garlic, finely chopped

Salt and freshly ground black
    pepper

1 pound cremini mushrooms,
    sliced

1 pound sourdough bread, cut
    into ½-inch dice (about 10 cups)

3 to 4 cups turkey or chicken
    broth

1 tablespoon finely chopped
    fresh marjoram

Preheat the oven to 350°F.

In a large skillet, melt the butter over medium-high heat. Add the sausage, break it into pieces, and cook until golden brown, about 7 minutes. Reduce the heat to medium, add the onions, celery, garlic, and a pinch of salt. Sauté, stirring frequently, for 5 minutes. Add the mushrooms and a pinch of salt and cook for 3 minutes.

Place the bread in a large bowl and stir in the sausage mixture. Add 3 cups of the broth and the marjoram and mix well (if the mixture is still dry, add a little more broth); season with salt and pepper. Butter a 9-by-11-inch baking dish. Transfer the stuffing to the dish, cover with foil, and bake for 15 minutes. Remove the foil and bake until the top is crisp and brown, about 45 minutes more.

LADLES The Deans love ladling and therefore own a proliferation of ladles. Soup, sauce, gravy, punch, and any other liquid that needs to be transported from one vessel to another, we ladle it.

GRAVY

TURKEY STOCK
Turkey neck and giblets (reserve
   the liver for the gravy)
Olive oil
3 carrots, coarsely chopped
3 ribs celery with tops
3 onions, chopped or quartered
10 whole black peppercorns

GRAVY
¼ cup turkey drippings
¼ cup flour
1½ cups dry vermouth
Turkey liver

MAKE THE TURKEY STOCK: In a small skillet, sauté the turkey neck and giblets in a bit of olive oil over medium-high heat until golden brown all over. Place a large stockpot over medium-high heat and fill three quarters of the way with water. Add the sautéed turkey neck and giblets, the carrots, celery, 2 of the chopped onions, and the peppercorns. Bring to a simmer and cook forever, while you set the table, polish the silver, give yourself a manicure, and drink a glass of wine. Some gray foam will form on top of the liquid, so skim this off when you see it.

After 4 to 6 hours, strain and discard the solids, except the turkey neck and heart. Strip the meat off the turkey neck and chop up the heart; reserve. (The stock can be made and refrigerated 1 day ahead.)

MAKE THE GRAVY: Take your turkey roasting pan (after transferring the roasted turkey to a platter), and pour off all the turkey drippings into a measuring cup. Return ¼ cup of the fat to the roasting pan, which still contains the leftover skin and fond. Using a spoon, discard the remaining clear fat from the measuring cup, which will have risen above the drippings. Set the roasting pan over medium heat and whisk in the flour, stirring up all the tasty bits at the bottom of the pan. Continue to cook until a dark brown roux has formed, 3 to 6 minutes. Add the drippings from the measuring cup and the vermouth.

Cook and stir until the bottom of the pan is "clean."

Transfer the mixture to a medium saucepan. Add the turkey stock and bring to a boil. In a small skillet, fry the liver in a bit of butter, dice it, and add to the gravy along with the reserved neck meat and chopped heart.

SEAFOOD FORK The Deans love seafood forks. Their shape, their arcaneness—we're not sure why, but we just love these little guys. Anything we can think of doing with them, we do, just as an excuse to get them out. We use them for shrimp cocktail and oysters on the half shell, of course. But we don't stop there. We employ them to pierce pickles on hamburger night and we always keep at least one in our purse to stab our husbands under the table in case they stray dangerously off topic or blatantly ignore all other hints that it is time to leave.

PORCELAIN OR SILVER BOWLS There is nothing in the world more elegant than a whole mousse—as opposed to individual portions—passed at the table for dessert. You will never see this done at a restaurant, and it is a real treat. Guests get to see the full majesty of your creation and in turn, you get the adulation that you so deserve. Giving guests control over their own serving ensures that sugar lovers can dig deep and pile high, and perpetual dieters can take their one little bite or less. When not being used, the bowl dresses up your dining table, sideboard, or front hall. This bowl is so beautiful that it needs no other adornment.

The following desserts can get you through all your entertaining.

CHOCOLATE COGNAC MOUSSE

SERVES 6

1 pound semisweet chocolate,
   cut into pieces
6 eggs, separated
¼ cups orange-flavored liqueur,
   such as Cointreau, or dark rum

½ cup sugar
Unsweetened whipped cream,
   for serving

In a double boiler, melt the chocolate over simmering water. Remove from the heat and stir in the egg yolks with a rubber spatula or wooden spoon (do not use a whisk). Stir in the liqueur.

Using a standing mixer fitted with the whisk attachment, beat the egg whites until stiff. Gradually beat in the sugar until stiff peaks form. Using a rubber spatula, thoroughly fold one-third of the egg whites into the chocolate mixture (this lightens the mixture). Gently fold in the remaining whites. Pour the mousse into your most decorative bowl. Refrigerate until firm, at least 2 hours or overnight.

When it's time to serve, pass the bowl of mousse around the table with a serving spoon and an accompanying bowl of whipped cream. The combination never fails to delight.

ANY-FOOL-CAN-MAKE-THIS FOOL

SERVES 4

1 pound strawberries, hulled

½ cup sugar

1 lemon, zested and juiced

1 teaspoon balsamic vinegar

1½ cups heavy cream

1 vanilla bean, seeds scraped

   (pod reserved for another use)

In a large saucepan, combine the strawberries, sugar, lemon zest, and lemon juice. Cook over medium heat, mashing the strawberries with the back of a fork until the strawberries are partially broken down and the sugar is melted, but it is not yet a puree. Refrigerate until cool, about 1 hour. Take it out of the refrigerator and stir in the balsamic vinegar.

In a large bowl, whip the cream with the vanilla bean seeds until stiff peaks form. Partially fold in the cold strawberry sauce, leaving a few contrasting scarlet and white steaks. Serve in a large bowl with a serving spoon.

COCKTAIL PARTIES:

A Goat Roping of Various and Sundry Acquaintances

"We're gonna to fight for our right to party!"

BEASTIE BOYS

Tinkling glasses, low light, trilling laughter—they're all irrefutable evidence of a cocktail party. A good cocktail party has a hum to it—it's sophisticated and relaxed at the same time. Maybe it's the word _cocktails_ or the spike heels, or perhaps it's the thought that you might spy a smoking jacket paired with velvet slippers? A cocktail party is a rite of passage for adults—no children here—and we're happy to see its resurgence.

LAST-MINUTE COCKTAIL PARTIES

A last-minute cocktail party is often the best kind. The reason is that the people who say yes are obviously in a party mood, and those who are not can easily beg off. You now have a celebratory group coming, and soon, but what's your plan? Have no fear; the Deans are here to give you the tools to throw an impromptu party whenever you wish. You can be the most versatile entertainer on your block.

How much lead-time have you given yourself? Forty-five minutes or a few hours? Don't worry; with our game plans you can do anything. Be creative and use whatever is on hand—let yourself get carried away. The anticipation can be more fun than the party itself!

1. FAST-AND-FURIOUS 45-MINUTE PLAN

PLAY PARTY music while you set up to solidify your party spirit.

STUFF DRINKS in the freezer for quick frosting.

GET ICE.

SET UP a dedicated bar area.

CUT UP lemons and limes—*there should be citrus on hand at all times.*

PREPARE THE FOOD. (*You only need olives and almonds. More is nice but not necessary for a quickie.*)

GET your powder room guest-ready.

CLIP GREENERY if you can. This is no time to be snobby—weeds fill a flower vase just as well as roses, each is chic in its own way.

DIM THE LIGHTS to the lowest possible setting. *A darkened room is far sexier.*

GET DRESSED well before start time. Some people get the time wrong and the Deans have been caught with their shirts off, literally.

HAND A DRINK to every guest the very second they arrive (*this is easy if you make a big batch of a specialty cocktail ahead of time*). The elixir will facilitate the guests' ideal buzz as soon as possible.

2. THE ALL-DAY PLAN

What a difference a day makes! With a whole day spread out before you, there's time to dream and then turn your dream into reality. Get out two recipes you have been dying to try—today's your day. Make the shopping the first chore. Go ahead and run the vacuum because we know you've been meaning to anyway. Set up your ironing board, turn on your favorite daytime talk show, and iron away: Ironed cocktail linens will make you feel battle-ready. Keep an eye on the clock because we don't want you to get too carried away and lose sight of the time. Leave the second-to-last hour for a bath and a dressing drink. Relaxing is essential to put you in a languid and fluid frame of mind, which in turn will put your guests at ease.

3. LONG-TERM PLAN

Many of you may feel intimated by hosting last-minute events. You may want more time. This section is for you. First, claim real estate on your friends' calendars. Holidays and springtime get busy so if you choose these times for a party, you'll want to get your invites out early. But too far in advance looks desperate. We recommend three to four weeks out. Much more lead time and people will forget.

A party planned this far in advance requires a hook: a friend visiting from out of town, your anniversary, your cat's birthday, Cinco de Mayo—you get the picture.

Invitations can be paper or paperless, but not by phone, because no one remembers a phone call a month later. A kickass invitation ignites anticipatory feeling and your event begins the moment the invitation is opened. A save-the-date card for a cocktail party, on the other hand, just puts a pit in the Deans' stomach. Instead of pleasant anticipation, we get a feeling that a prison sentence awaits us. Unless the event is going to be off-the-charts exciting, a save-the-date card is pretentious. We hope we have struck the initial blow in killing this practice.

Now, let's decide who you are inviting. You are going to want to cast a wide-ish net, because 66 percent of invitees will be available, always. This is the

math. Why does it work this way? Did you argue with your algebra teacher? So, don't argue with us. Sixty-six percent will say yes.

One way to make your local town feel twice as big and three times as fun is to ask ten friends to each bring a new guest or couple. At the party, each friend is responsible for introducing their guest. Put all of them in a relatively tight space so that they mingle and mix maximally.

With weeks to prepare, there is no excuse not to push yourself in some new direction. Make an outstanding specialty drink with a novelty liquor, cover a banister with crepe paper and fairy lights, line your walkway with candles in glass votives. No detail needs to be difficult or wildly expensive; it just needs to deviate from the expected. Your guests will love the attention you have lavished on them.

Begin your doting when they enter the front door. Just as you may be nervous to be hosting a party, your guests may be nervous going to one. A warm, generous welcome puts guests at ease and makes them feel glad they left their house. A hearty hello while plying your guests liberally with cocktails will get your party humming in no time. Make sure the first drink is within easy reach.

THE COCKTAIL BUFFET

In a class by itself stands the cocktail buffet. Definition: a party halfway between a standing cocktail party and a seated buffet supper.

This type of party requires work and planning, so we don't host them often, but sometimes it's the perfect solution for what we crave.

The Deans consider a cocktail buffet a large party, twenty to eighty guests. Hosts and guests have a few options with this event. The guests get to

"The lifeblood of the party flows from the bar and people must be able to see it at all times."

decide whether they want to make their visit a pit stop en route somewhere else, or their final resting place for the evening. The host entertains many people in a generous but loose style. This is the moment to swoop up people on the outer fringes of your acquaintance. Your guests can move around and talk to as many people as they want for as long as they wish, unlike at a seated dinner party. As opposed to a standing cocktail party, they can sit down and engage in deep conversations.

This is a carefree party with no hard-and-fast rules, so your interpretation is ready to be stamped upon the evening. If you have always pictured your house as a souk or Mexican cantina, for instance, now is the time to satisfy your multiple personalities. Of course, lively music adds to the festivity (no dirges, please). In other words, if you crave structure, this may not be your ideal event, but if you have a creative streak and lots of energy, the cocktail buffet is your baby!

One rule: The bar should be immediately visible to the party guest. Never obstruct the bar with a Christmas tree or tuck it behind a staircase or anything else. The lifeblood of the party flows from the bar and people must be able to see it at all times. If you are going to have a bartender, hire a hottie— easier on the eyes for all.

If the drinks and food are difficult to access and far away from each other, the party will never ignite. People fruitlessly roam around trying to find the nonexistent action. If you have to close doors or put certain rooms off limits, do that. People want to be able to see each other, even if they are packed like sardines.

The cocktail buffet can incorporate some splashy effects. You can't be surprised to hear the Deans have an opinion about how to dress for the cocktail parties. An elaborate hostess gown is de rigueur. If you have three or four small brooches, arrange them all together (one alone emits a small squeak, while a bunch heralds a celebratory mood). If your cocktail buffet looks like it may become an annual event, we suggest investing in an outfit that is timeless, elegant, and outstanding (brocade, velvet, lace). After you worked so hard, slipping into something scrumptious makes you feel like all your work was worthwhile.

The cocktail buffet is perfect for your shoe-loving girlfriends. They can teeter in on their highest heels in full effect, but the minute their feet start to ache they can sit down and those shoes can dangle like jewels in front of everyone's face.

A revelry of this scope can accommodate up to three specialty drinks and a myriad of different cocktail foods. Provide enough food so that no one needs to go out afterward, and have many things from which to choose. Present both finger foods and several heartier dishes for your hungrier guests. Serve them on your little plates that you may have contemplated throwing out (more on this weighty topic in the holiday section). Some people will want to load up and sit down, while others will want to pick at things and flit from friend to friend.

Here are some cocktail buffet food tips to get you started:

* **NOBODY WANTS A FINGER FOOD** that looks like it's too much of a commitment, especially when they have a drink in the their other hand. Feel free to mix and match passed foods with your buffet items. Just be sure that the finger foods are one bite only.

* **HAVE ONE LARGE PROTEIN** (ham, beef tenderloin, turkey) with small pieces of soft white bread accompanied with mayo and mustard so people can make little sandwiches. An entire side of smoked fish is another good choice. Serve it with slices of brown bread and chopped red onions, capers, and lemon wedges.

* **BABY CARROTS ARE NOT FOOD**, they are slimy and gross, and furthermore, they are not baby carrots. They are adult carrots whittled down by a machine. Please don't express astonishment that your bowl of baby carrots was not eaten. Buy a full-size carrot and slice it if carrots are what you want. Similarly, a stingy little piece of celery cannot be elevated with a dab of Boursin or, God forbid, peanut butter. No one wants to eat celery stuffed with anything. Raw broccoli should live on the compost heap—its woody, fibrous texture is no friend to merry making.

THE DEANS' FAVORITE COCKTAIL SNACKS

Richard Avedon said style is based on repetition, not duplication. All you need are a few signature recipes and drinks—then own them. No need to reinvent the wheel every time you entertain. People will look forward to your specialty. Have you ever made a playlist? Make a recipe list. Here is ours.

SALMON CANAPÉS

These take two seconds to make, less if you have your middle-schooler do them. Be sure to use Scottish or Atlantic smoked salmon and pile it generously on each sandwich. A few hearty sandwiches are far more palatable than multiple anorexic ones. If you serve only this hors d'oeuvre, guests will feel they have been showered with love. *MAKES 20 GENEROUS CANAPÉS*

One 17.6-ounce package pumpernickel bread (we prefer Mestemacher Natural with whole rye kernels)
8 ounces crème fraîche
8 ounces smoked Atlantic salmon, sliced thin
1 lemon
2 tablespoons capers
Freshly ground black pepper

Cut the bread into triangles. Smear crème fraîche on each slice and pile high with the salmon. Drizzle with the juice from the lemon and top with the capers. Capers will roll off and serve double duty as décor and garnish. Sprinkle with the pepper.

GOUGÈRES

This cheese puff recipe circumnavigates the globe ten times a year. Every well-heeled host knows about them, and every hungry party guest longs for them. If you haven't already, it's high time you've added these to your arsenal. If they have slipped your mind lately, the Deans are pleased to reacquaint you with them. The French name and the directions sound daunting, but nothing could be further from the truth. These feathery puffs are so delicate, yet they can anchor any festivity. One cup water, one cup flour, one cup cheese: Let's all count to one and make *gougères*. *MAKES 40*

1 cup water
8 tablespoons butter
1 cup flour

1 cup grated Gruyère or cheddar
Cracked black pepper
4 eggs

Preheat the oven to 425°F.

In a medium saucepan, bring the water and butter to a boil over high heat until the butter is melted. Immediately pour in all the flour and stir for 1 minute over medium heat to evaporate the excess water (even though the dough may seem a bit dry, don't skip this step).

Transfer the dough ball to a food processor or standing mixer (strangely, either one works for this recipe). Add the cheese and several generous twists of pepper. With the machine on, add the eggs and mix until incorporated.

Using two small spoons, scoop 2 teaspoons of dough at a time, forming a ball. Drop the balls as you make them onto nonstick baking sheet, spacing well apart because these guys are going to puff up. Bake until golden and puffed, 20 to 25 minutes. Serve immediately.

Once the *gougères* are cold, they are stale, so do not bake them all at once. If you are having a cocktail party, put the *gougères* dough on the baking sheets before start time, and put one tray at a time in the oven so that your *gougères* are always served warm.

STEAK BITES

Steak bites are the perfect last-minute cocktail snack. You can always find a steak on sale, and these bites are a cinch to make. *MAKES 10 TO 12 BITES*

1½ pounds New York strip steak, at room temperature

Sea salt and freshly ground black pepper
Vegetable oil

Preheat the oven to 350°F.

Evenly and generously coat both sides of the steaks with sea salt and pepper. Heat a large, heavy skillet over medium heat. Add the oil (or, better yet, cut a bit of fat from the steak and melt it in the pan). Add the steaks and sear until a crust forms, 2 to 3 minutes. Flip the steaks and place the pan in the oven. Roast for 3 to 8 minutes to desired doneness. Transfer to a plate and let rest for 15 minutes.

Trim and discard any gristle and fat and cut the meat into bite-size cubes. Serve on forks or skewers, sprinkled with a little more sea salt.

HAM & PIMIENTO DEVILED EGGS

If you enter the Academy kitchen and see the pilot light off, and the Deans nowhere to be found, there is a good chance they have opted for lunch at the Butcher and Bee. Everything served at this establishment is worth trying and the ambience is low-key and relaxed. Its quirky hours—11 a.m. to 3 p.m. and 11 p.m. to 3 a.m.—appeal to our sense of the bizarre. We tapped Butcher and Bee for their deviled egg recipe because these eggs are so good sometimes we've been known to throw ourselves out of bed at 1 a.m. to go fetch one.

Deviled eggs should be served right away, but do not take long to put together. You can keep the filling and whites separate, however, to extend the make-ahead time (no more than 1 day in advance, though), as long as everything is kept chilled. *MAKES 6 HORS D'OEUVRES*

6 eggs, preferably not farm fresh (fresh eggs don't peel well!)

1 ounce mayonnaise (we like Dukes or Kewpie)

2 teaspoons smooth Dijon mustard

2 teaspoons pickle juice (bread-and-butter-pickle juice, if you have it)

1 red bell pepper, roasted, peeled, seeded, and finely chopped

2 ounces deli ham, finely diced

1 teaspoon finely chopped fresh parsley

Hot sauce and coarse salt, for seasoning

In a large saucepan, combine the eggs and enough water to cover by 2 inches. Bring to a boil, then remove from the heat. Let the eggs sit in the hot water for 8 minutes, then transfer to an ice bath to stop the cooking process.

Gently roll the eggs on a flat surface to crack the shells. Peel the eggs and halve them lengthwise. Remove the yolks and place in a small bowl. Add the remaining ingredients, seasoning to your liking with the hot sauce and salt. Spoon the yolk mixture back into the whites, and serve right away or refrigerate and serve chilled.

BACON-WRAPPED DELIGHTS 1.0:
PRUNES WRAPPED IN BACON

These prunes are blast-furnace hot when they come out of the oven, so do not pop one in your mouth immediately, or you will have created a medical emergency. *MAKES 24 HORS D'OEUVRES*

24 pitted prunes

12 thin slices bacon, halved
crosswise

Preheat the broiler and position the rack two levels from the top.

Wrap each prune with a half piece of bacon. Broil for 2 to 3 minutes per side until the bacon is crisp. Using tongs, transfer to a platter. Let cool for 5 minutes before serving.

BACON-WRAPPED DELIGHTS 2.0:
ANGELS ON HORSEBACK

The name alone connotes guardian angels battling the Four Horsesmen of the Apocalypse. And to think of that going on in your own living room! If your guests do not go insane upon seeing deep-fried oysters with bacon, then you need new friends. What an outrageous treat and you are a phenom for having provided such a luxury snack. Only you and the Deans will know how easy they are to create. *MAKES 24 HORS D'OEUVRES*

Vegetable oil, preferably
peanut oil
2 dozen oysters, shucked

Pour enough oil in a deep saucepan to reach a depth of at least 3 inches. Heat the oil to 375°F on a deep-fat thermometer. Wrap each oyster with a half piece of bacon and secure with a toothpick.

12 thin slices bacon, halved
crosswise

Add the oysters in batches to the hot oil and fry until the bacon is crisp, 2 to 3 minutes. Using a slotted spoon, transfer the oysters to a paper towel to drain. Serve hot.

CANDIED BACON

Remember that commercial where the dog runs around muttering "bacon, bacon, bacon"? It turns out that party guests are the same. Bacon's heady aroma is so enticing that the Deans assure you: Two or three bacon appetizers are not overkill. *SERVES 12*

½ pound of your favorite sliced bacon

Turbinado sugar or light brown sugar

Freshly cracked black pepper

Cayenne

Preheat the oven to 350°F.

Halve the bacon slices crosswise and arrange on parchment-lined baking sheets so that the pieces don't touch. Sprinkle the sugar liberally on top to cover the bacon; season with black pepper and cayenne to taste. Bake, rotating once, until the sugar is caramelized, about 20 minutes.

A TREASURE TROVE OF CHEESE COINS

At Christmas time, the Deans receive a cruel lashing from friends if we attend any event without bearing canvas bags overflowing with cheese coins. They are the Academy's signature treats and Dean Manigault's muscled right arm is a testament that the cheddar is lovingly grated by hand. Sometimes this can mean up to 25 pounds of cheddar because we have so many friends and students to bestow coins upon. *MAKES ABOUT 2 DOZEN*

16 ounces shredded sharp cheddar

2 sticks (8 ounces) unsalted butter, cut into 8 pieces

2 cups unbleached flour

1 heaping teaspoon cayenne

22 twists freshly ground black pepper

½ teaspoon salt

Using a standing mixer or food processor, whirl all the ingredients until combined. Form the cheese dough into 2 logs, about 1½ inches in diameter. Wrap in plastic wrap and refrigerate for at least 2 hours and up to 3 days (or freeze for up to 6 weeks).

Preheat the oven to 325°F.

Cut the logs into ¼-inch slices and place on baking sheets. Bake for 18 to 20 minutes, until golden brown. Serve warm or at room temperature (or let cool and store in airtight containers for up to 7 days).

SPICY BAR NUTS

Check out any local bar and notice what the snack of choice is. Nothing gets past the Deans. Be sure to serve these with paper cocktail napkins. *MAKES ABOUT 4 CUPS*

1 stick (4 ounces) butter

2 tablespoons cajun spice

1 tablespoon ground turmeric

1 teaspoon cayenne

2 pounds mixed cashews, pecans, almonds, and walnuts

In a large skillet, melt the butter over medium heat. Stir in the spices. Pour in the nuts and scrape up from the bottom of the pan with a spatula until the nuts are evenly coated and the spices are thoroughly distributed, about 4 minutes. Serve warm or at room temperature. (The nuts will keep in an airtight container for several days.)

"Pour yourself a glass."

THE DEANS' FAVORITE COCKTAILS

You'll never read Milton's *Paradise Lost* if you don't know your ABCs; you can't become an engineer if you don't master rudimentary math. Every leader in the arts, from Picasso to Louis Armstrong to Baryshnikov, understood that basic technique must be learned before inventive improvisation is feasible. Similarly, no one creates first-class cocktails unless they have conquered the four bedrock drinks of all mixology, one for rum, bourbon, vodka, and tequila. Since you already can open a bottle of wine, pour yourself a glass and let the Deans walk you through the sophisticated, elegant, and timeless hard-liquor drinks. This officially signals your passage into adulthood. For good measure, we've also included a classic Champagne Cocktail.

Please note that the Deans measure in cups and tablespoons, not ounces, because those confuse us, so we assume they confuse you, too. You can't get far with cocktails unless you have a batch of simple syrup on hand. This liquid sugar makes sweetening drinks a snap. It's easy to prepare, and can be stored for up to a month.

SIMPLE SYRUP

MAKES ¾ CUP

½ cup sugar

½ cup water

In a small saucepan, heat the sugar and water together over medium heat. Stir continuously until all the sugar is dissolved. Let cool, then pour into a jar and refrigerate until needed.

RUM: THE DAIQUIRI

When you want to get happy, frisky, and flirty, rum is your poison. The high sugar content combined with the alcohol packs a double whammy. Several sips of a frou-frou, frothy, lime-infused concoction and you'll be giggling and seducing just like Marilyn Monroe herself. *MAKES 1 DRINK*

2 ounces (¼ cup) light rum (Cruzan Rum is our favorite)

¾ to 1 ounce (⅛ cup) fresh lime juice

½ ounce (1 tablespoon) Simple Syrup (see opposite)

2 drops Angostura bitters (optional—if you are feeling in the mood for a pink ladies' drink riff)

Ice cubes

In a cocktail shaker, shake the rum, lime juice, simple syrup, and bitters, if using. Strain into a cocktail glass filled with large ice cubes, and stir.

A TANKFUL OF RUM DAIQUIRIS

SERVES 8

1½ cups white rum (preferably Cruzan)

1 cup fresh lime juice

⅔ cup Simple Syrup (see opposite)

Crushed ice

Ice cubes

1 lime, sliced

In a large bowl, pour the rum, lime juice, and simple syrup over crushed ice. Stir vigorously. Strain into cocktail glasses filled with large ice cubes. Float a slice of lime on each drink. Refrigerate extra daiquiri.

BOURBON: THE OLD-FASHIONED

Bourbon is the oil that keeps the gears of Southern society well lubricated. The big brown liquors are bold and it takes practice and diligence before they become palatable. Serving the big browns says no children will be joining us. These drinks must be sipped slowly, so strong are they, and they spark conversations and relationships in equal order. Here you can use rye or bourbon. Serve in a traditional Old-Fashioned glass, which is short and wide with a heavy bottom. *MAKES 1 DRINK*

1 large slice of lemon peel
(or, if you want to be more
traditional, orange peel)
1½ teaspoons Simple Syrup
(see page 138)
2 dashes Angostura bitters

1 dash Regan's Orange Bitters
No. 6
Large ice cubes
2 ounces (¼ cup) rye or bourbon
1 maraschino cherry, preferably
Luxardo

In an Old-Fashioned glass, combine the lemon peel, simple syrup, and both bitters. Muddle with the back of a spoon to crush the lemon peel and release its oils. You don't have to get too precious about muddling because once the bourbon hits these ingredients almost all other flavors are obliterated.

Add the ice and then the bourbon.

As if this drink wasn't super glam enough, we float one cherry on the top. It may sink to the bottom but where it sinks after floating is its own business. Stir with a spoon.

"Bourbon is the oil that keeps the gears of Southern society well lubricated."

AN ONSLAUGHT OF OLD-FASHIONEDS

When anticipating a thirsty hoard, the Deans find that pre-making Old-Fashioneds in batches saves time. We sprinkle in the bitters at the end to provide a loving touch, but otherwise the work is complete. Have a supply of speciality ice cubes on hand—if you are not creating bespoke ice cubes by now, you are woefully behind all current cultural trends. *SERVES 12*

Ice cubes

One 750-ml bottle rye or
    bourbon

¼ cup Simple Syrup (see page 138)

¼ cup cold water

12 dashes orange bitters,
    preferably blood orange

24 dashes Angostura bitters

12 large slice of lemon peel

12 maraschino cherries,
    preferably Luxardo

Fill a silver pitcher a quarter full of ice. Pour in the rye or bourbon. Stir in the simple syrup and water. Pour the mixture into ice cube–filled glasses.

One dash orange bitters, 2 dashes Angostura bitters, a lemon peel, and a cherry complete each drink.

VODKA: THE BLOODY MARY

If mac and cheese can be one of the vegetables on "a meat and three" buffet, then the Deans assert that the Bloody Mary is a salad. This bloody is just as tasty virgin, by the way. *MAKES 1 DRINK*

Ice cubes

2 ounces (¼ cup) vodka

¾ cup Clamato

½ teaspoon grated fresh or
    prepared horseradish

4 dashes Worcestershire sauce

3 dashes Tabasco sauce

¼ teaspoon celery salt

Old Bay seasoning

1 lemon wedge, dilly bean,
    or pickled okra, for garnish

Over ice, pour all the ingredients in a glass. Stir vigorously. Top with several shakes of Old Bay and garnish with a lemon wedge, dilly bean, or pickled okra.

A BEVY OF BLOODIES

SERVES 16

One 64-ounce bottle Clamato

Grated fresh horseradish or bot-
    tled horseradish

Worcestershire sauce

Tabasco sauce

Celery salt

32 ounces (4 cups) vodka

Ice cubes

Old Bay seasoning

Lemon wedges, dilly beans,
    and pickled okra, for garnish

Pour the Clamato into a pitcher. Add heaping helpings of horseradish, Worcestershire, Tabasco, and celery salt to taste. The Deans find more is more.

Pour 2 ounces vodka per drink over ice cubes and fill the rest of the glass with the Clamato mixture. Top with several shakes of Old Bay, which provides a savory floater that takes this Bloody Mary over the top. Garnish each drink with a lemon wedge, dilly bean, and pickled okra. Dean-licious.

TEQUILA: THE MARGARITA

Beware of the Margarita. The most delicious and authentic only have lime juice, tequila, and Cointreau. Two liquors hide in them there waters and make no mistake, even if your mind forgets they are there, your body won't. Two of these may well be one too many. *MAKES 1 DRINK*

Salt, for rimming the glass (optional)
Ice cubes
2 ounces (¼ cup) tequila, preferably 100% agave

1½ ounces (3 tablespoons) fresh lime juice
⅛ ounce (½ teaspoon) Cointreau

If you like salt on your Margarita, place the salt in a shallow dish. Rub the cut side of a lime around the rim of the cocktail glass, then dip in the salt.

Fill a cocktail shaker with ice. Pour in the tequila, lime juice, and Cointreau and shake away. Either serve straight up or over more ice in cocktail glasses.

MUCHAS MARGARITAS

SERVES 6

1½ cups tequila
½ cup Cointreau

1 cup fresh lime juice
Ice cubes

Combine all the ingredients in a pitcher and stir vigorously. Pour into cocktail glasses and serve straight up or over ice.

CHAMPAGNE: THE CHAMPAGNE COCKTAIL

This libation is the only beverage that slakes your thirst for romance. Champagne cries out for a mate, for you and for itself. While it is of course delicious alone, it happily settles into a marriage with various fruits and additives. The Champagne Cocktail is elegant and celebratory as all get-out. One is fun, but while we are at it, why don't we make a whole punch-bowl full and invite a few people in? *MAKES 1 DRINK*

5 dashes Angostura bitters
1 sugar cube
Champagne

In a champagne flute, dash the bitters over a sugar cube. Top with Champagne.

CHAMPAGNE PUNCH

You can make your own ice block in a mold using pear juice, embed raspberries or other colorful fruits in the ice. When the juice-flavored ice block melts, it only improves the flavor. *SERVES 16*

4 bottles champagne or
    prosecco, chilled
1 bottle (750 ml) pear nectar,
    such as Looza, chilled
1½ cups Poire William liqueur,
    chilled
Ice block or ice cubes

Combine all the ingredients in a large punch bowl. Serve in flutes.

QUALITY ICE ALL THE TIME.

Ice from the supermarket will suffice for large parties but in general it is not satisfactory. It melts quickly, tastes bad, looks ugly: a trifecta of horrors. If your icemaker is not up to snuff, make a pile of cubes ahead of time and freeze in bags.

EMERGENCY FROZEN PARTY FOODS AND SALTED NUTS.

Pigs in a blanket, mini quiches, and spanakopita are never going to mark you as the most sophisticated host on the planet. On the other hand, their asset lies in their familiarity and the fact that they are universally liked. For a last-minute party, expectations are lowered and tasty well-known food will be a welcome sight to all. Keeping a pack of frozen comestibles on hand takes a bit of stress away from having unexpected guests. With a heated treat and some salted nuts, you can entertain anyone at the drop of a hat.

PART III

MASTER
CLASS

*"The Deans dedicate an afternoon—sipping a Champagne
Cocktail—while meeting in the Academy war room."*

THE HOLIDAYS:

Hit a Home Run

CIRCUMVENTING STRIFE

We went to a lot of trouble and expense, have been planning for months, cooking for days: Why aren't we having any fun? A comprehensive plan for the entire holiday will pull you through the season, so spend time making a good one. The Deans dedicate an afternoon—sipping a Champagne Cocktail (see page 144) and eating a lunch of Scalloped Oysters (see next page)—while meeting in the Academy war room. General Patton could have taken a lesson from the Deans in getting his division battle-ready.

Our first hard-and-fast rule is that the start time of the main event for all major holidays has to be in the afternoon. Evening is just too late— the chances of major drama ensuing go up exponentially. After an afternoon meal, on the other hand, everyone still has some energy left for games, reading, cleanup, and relaxation.

Simplify your plan before you even start by disabusing yourself of the notion that everybody needs hors d'oeuvres on the big day. Hors d'oeuvres are pointless for the holidays. If you don't understand why, the Deans say leave class until you can figure it out.

SCALLOPED OYSTERS

Perfect for your holiday meal as a side dish, or paired with a salad as a light lunch for when people drop by. *SERVES 3 TO 4*

3 cloves garlic, finely chopped
1 tablespoon unsalted butter
2 pints oysters
½ cup white wine
½ cup heavy cream

5 Ritz crackers
2 tablespoons grated Parmesan
Salt and freshly ground black
    pepper

Preheat the broiler.

Sprinkle the garlic in a 9-by-13-inch casserole dish. Add the butter and run it under the broiler to melt. Remove from the oven.

Add the oysters, white wine, and cream to the casserole dish. Crumble the crackers on top and stir briefly to combine. Top with the Parmesan; season with salt and pepper.

Broil until hot and bubbly, but not burned, 5 to 10 minutes. Keep an eye on the dish because anything under a broiler can burn quickly. Serve at once.

SHOPPING SPREE

You are going to thank us forever when we give you this tip: Grocery shop first thing in the morning during the holidays. Getting to the supermarkets first thing in the morning will ensure that the aisles are crowd free and lines have not had time to form at the register. Other benefits are that your spouse can enjoy an extra cup of coffee with your children, and you have maximum energy with which to shop. If you are anticipating large numbers, going to the store for four or five days in a row breaks the shopping down into manageable amounts. Lists are crucial at this time of year for stable mental health, since you are being pulled in nine thousand directions and you will *not* remember everything you need to buy. Just like Santa himself, you need to check those lists twice, possibly three times, and keep a pad of paper nearby for constant editing. In the dappled sun of early morning you will zip up and down the aisles, unfettered and free, while later, your tardy neighbors will be hunched over their carts, their misery radiating off of them like a hot star.

DOING THE DISHES

Paper plates for a holiday meal are not acceptable, except when they are. When you have too many other things going on and you know that cleaning the dishes will ruin everyone's experience, including your own, pull out some paper plates. No one knows better than the Deans how exhausting the experience of hosting relatives can be, especially when you throw in several toddlers. Trying to be mother, daughter, and best friend at once guarantees that you will be stretched and contorted close to the breaking point. And since there's no scrimping on the holiday meal—no hamburger, mac and cheese, or cereal—for this gang, if serving the meal on paper plates is going to get you through the day with sanity, then the Deans heartily endorse chinette. It's your holiday, so do what you must, and we promise to bring the good attitude. But may we ask, sotto vocce, that you at least get plates with a pretty pattern and not the white paper ones that disintegrate at the sight of the turkey?

Don't do anything rash with your china. The Deans are all about staying lean and getting rid of clutter, but hesitate before off-loading your good dishes just because you haven't used them for a while. Circumstances change and dinnerware is expensive, so if you cast off your china, there is a good chance you won't replace it. Hold on—you won't have toddlers forever, your elderly relatives will move on to greener pastures, and one night you may find yourself longing for your good plates to remind you and your husband that you are attuned to the finer things in life.

THE PASSING OF THE TOQUE

You've all seen *Downton Abbey* and noticed that the Granthams have copious staff. Perhaps you haven't noticed that you have staff, too. And, good news, they are live-in. If you have children, you have helpers. They are difficult to train, crabby, and not necessarily very good, just like all staff, but these people exist and should be indoctrinated accordingly. The Deans have noticed too many children sitting by like pashas of a bygone era while their mothers run around to the point of exhaustion waiting on everyone. These children need to learn to pitch in.

"If you have children, you have helpers."

The best reason to give birth to sons is to hand over every labor-intensive job: frying a turkey, roasting a pig, moving the dining table and chairs, and peeling chestnuts. Do not let sons shirk away from these duties. These are manly activities that will fuel their testosterone, cause them to feel vital and lessen your workload to boot. Now that you are so relaxed from all the help, perhaps you and your spouse will have time to make a few more elves!

HOW TO FRY A TURKEY

In Charleston, fried turkey is a ubiquitous holiday offering. If you've never eaten a fried turkey, this year is the time to rectify the situation. Sons revel at the idea of taking charge, playing with fire, and providing food for their family. For those with no backyard or a patio, don't be afraid to appropriate street corners. Hunting for the perfect frying spot can be half the fun.

This outdoor activity requires that you purchase a dedicated turkey fryer—a metal stand attached to a propane tank, over which a large cauldron full of hot oil is placed. The turkey is lowered into said oil for a little under an hour. Tips number one and two are making sure your bird is completely dry and has been brought to room temperature before immersing it in the oil. Tips number three to ten: Never abandon your bird. Frying is much faster than roasting, so you are only going to need 45 minutes, but you will need to adjust the flame throughout as the oil temperature fluctuates. Although you are going to cook the bird at 350°F, you want the initial oil temperature to be 400°F to insure maximum crispness of skin. The oil temperature will drop when the bird enters the oil. Now your job is to keep watch over the thermometer and adjust the flame. Too high and you risk burning the bird, too low and your bird will emerge greasy.

It pains the Deans that we only see turkey at Thanksgiving and Christmas. This versatile bird is squawking for more table time. Fourth of July and Labor Day are ideal occasions for fried turkey. Your only issue is that you will not be able to procure a fresh turkey, so you will have to plan a few days ahead to defrost your frozen one. Once you've fried one turkey, we know you will fry another.

3 gallons peanut or other vegetable oil
One 13- to 18-pound turkey

Heat the oil to 400°F, following the directions on your turkey fryer.

Carefully lower the turkey into the oil and fry for 3½ minutes per pound. Remove the turkey, letting the excess oil drip off, then transfer to a cutting board. Let the turkey rest for 10 to 20 minutes before carving.

HOW TO SERVE FORTH FROM THE SEA

Boys in the low country start sport fishing as soon as they are able. They learn how to catch, clean, cook, and present to their family the bounty of the sea or lakes. The following recipe is an easy one for your family members to cut their teeth on—girls, too! (Yes, this recipe works as well with a storebought fish.)

SERVES 4

¾ cup flour

4 fresh fish steaks, such as mackerel, cobia, grouper, wahoo, or mahi-mahi

3 tablespoons olive oil

6 tablespoons butter

3 limes, halved

4 bunches scallions, trimmed

Put the flour on a large plate. Lightly coat both sides of the fish in the flour. In a large skillet, heat the olive oil over medium-high heat. Add the fish and sauté, turning once, until very crisp, about 10 minutes. Transfer the fish to a plate to rest.

Melt the butter in the pan, and squeeze in the juice from the limes. Sauté the whole scallions in the lime butter until wilted. Return the fish to the pan, and flip to coat with the lime butter. Sprinkle with sea salt.

TEN EASY STEPS TO PULLED PORK
FOR SERVING 50 TO 100 OF YOUR CLOSEST FRIENDS

Dean Pollak is such a fan of barbecued pork that she created her own pit master, son Christopher Pollak. The following are Christopher's exact directions for perfect pig, which he follows to the letter every time. Smoking a whole pig is a lengthy process so it's best to start at 8 or 9 p.m. and plan to stay up all night. This is not a one-man job. Two or more pit masters are required to keep all pit masters awake.

STEP 1:
Beg, borrow, or steal a smoker.

STEP 2:
Procure an 80- to 120-pound pig.

STEP 3:
Crack open your first beer; it's going to be a long night.

STEP 4:
Rest, with a cold beer.

STEP 5:
Light the smoker, and when the temperature is constant, place the pig
inside and keep the temperature at 225°F.

STEP 6:
Hydrate the pig with an apple-cider-vinegar-based mop sauce
every time you crack open a new beer.

STEP 7:
When the pig's internal temperature reaches 190°F, remove it from
the heat and let it rest. The total cooking time is roughly 10 hours,
plus or minus an hour or two.

STEP 8:
Perambulate with the pig around the perimeter of the party
to exhibit pride of pig.

STEP 9:
Pull (shred) the pig yourself or let guests pull the pig and serve themselves.

STEP 10:
Save the pig cheek for yourself to enjoy with a cold beer.
You deserve it.

A STRONG FINISH

The Deans don't know one cook alive who is not disheartened that the holiday meal takes four days to plan, four days to shop for, three days to cook, and ten minutes to eat. Just when the weary chef is ready to sit in the chair and bask in all her glory, the youngest participant pipes up, "May I be excused?" and the eldest starts corralling people to the car to go to the movies. How can this be happening? Including some adults who are not your immediate family can circumvent this travesty. Holidays are a good time to look around and realize that although you have a bounty of people coming to your house, some people are alone. Invite over two or three strays. They will keep your family on better behavior, and make your dinner an altogether jollier activity. Grateful guests are not looking to jump up from your table any more than you wish them to. Let the tiny children be excused, pour an extra glass of wine for everyone, put the turkey and pies somewhere within easy reach so everyone can keep picking and partying. We guarantee that your meal will be extended for a satisfactory amount of time.

PARLOR GAMES

The Deans posit that there are better ideas than plopping in front of the TV or going to a movie during the holidays. Parlor games, readings, and music playing were all skills that were honed when we couldn't plug in. Marie Antoinette probably would have tweeted and played Angry Birds if she could have, but whist was the game of the day and so that's what she played. Charades unites multiple ages. If you are plucky, here's an idea we can put up your sleeve, which might become a tradition. If you have a favorite essay, story, or poem, consider gathering everyone together and reading it aloud. Dean Manigault brings her entire Christmas party to tears by reading Truman Capote's *Christmas Memory*, a truly beautiful story. And never forget that good old-fashioned Monopoly hasn't been around for one hundred years because it isn't fun.

"Marie Antoinette probably would have tweeted and played Angry Birds if she could have."

THE CLEANUP

The Deans can't find a way around this fact of life: Once you've hosted a lavish friend-and-family-filled Thanksgiving or Christmas, your kitchen will look like a Category Five hurricane has just passed through. Multiple courses, multiple people, and multiple desserts means maximum mess. You will be far too resentful if you alone have to clean up for twenty-one people. This is not a one-man job. Consider hiring a helper, if possible. This is not an extravagance, since your money will be working double time: It will stimulate the economy as well as ease your lower back and your mind. Of course, hiring someone is not always possible. Fortunately, the Deans have noticed every large group has at least one good cleaner-upper. Choose a couple of guests who you know will not break all the china and ask them to help. They should be happy to oblige.

BE OUR GUEST

Just because you've been invited for a holiday meal does not mean you get to show up last minute looking gorgeous and hand the host a bunch of flowers or one bottle of wine and still retain the expectation that you will be invited back ever again. Maybe dish duty is not your calling, but find out what help is wanted far in advance. Enjoy buying wine? Offer to bring a case. A Thanksgiving or Christmas dinner is worthy of at least a half, if not a whole case of wine. If you know how to carve the turkey (and most people don't) go ahead and offer as soon as you are invited. A host's mind is eased by jobs that he can mentally check off. If there are any children around, the guest who can organize a touch football game, or any outdoor activity, becomes a star of the afternoon.

When Dean Pollak's son, Charles, was thirteen years old, her neighbor taught him to create a centerpiece, now one of her favorite holiday memories. Not only was the table beautiful, but also her young son learned the important art of gracious living. Be creative with your help as long as your offering is generous of spirit.

Do not be critical when you are a guest. The Deans have hosted decades of holiday meals and have served every traditional meal they could think of—geese, turkey, prime rib, ham, rack of lamb, cassoulet—but some of the most fun we have had is when we have gone to other people's houses where we marvel at their holiday meal interpretations. We relax because we are the guest for once and enjoy getting into someone else's flow. Guests have work to do, too, and that is being enthusiastic and upbeat about all that is on offer.

Traveling over the holidays is exhausting. There must be no supposition that the travelers can cook and do chores on the day of travel. It may look like they are swanning in at the last moment but anyone who has traveled by airplane recently knows that all vestige of glamour has been completely eradicated from this mode of transportation. Today you need to wear breakaway pants and slip-on shoes so you can perform your striptease for the TSA officers, after which you are shuttled to the cattle pen to wait for your flight to be canceled during the next three time slots. The only things worse than air travel are all the other options: endless hours in traffic with everyone in the car needing a pit stop and no one agreeing on music.

"The Deans read somewhere that tensions can run higher around the holidays."

The person hosting naturally bears the greatest burden of the cooking and cleaning. Hosts must hold no resentment about their extra onus and guests must be grateful for everything provided for them. This applies to all events, but the Deans read somewhere that tensions can run higher around the holidays. Make sure you are treading lightly.

FAMILY TRADITIONS

Holiday menus are major emotional triggers. Couples will hit the mat about their family traditions and "the way we did it at our house." If your wife always went to the six o'clock service, believe the Deans, you are going, too. For the newly married this can be a minefield. Our advice is to try and start your own traditions. Go gently at first and pull a few items from both family rituals. No one will die if they are pressed into mashing potatoes or forced into eating Brussels sprouts. The Deans know for certain that too many expectations applied for a big event is a guarantee for disaster. The word *perfect* must be banished from your holiday vocabulary.

When these expectations are not met, feelings get hurt and resentment is born. Communication is vital. Tempers flare when plans are made that are disregarded or ignored. Hosts and guests equally share the responsibility of laying out all their hopes and dreams for the duration of the stay. Both sides must compromise so that there is ample time together as well as space apart. Hosts do not like to feel they are running a hotel and guests do not like to be micromanaged. Call well before you arrive and ask your host what activities he absolutely expects to see you attend, and lob out the ideas you have. If the hosts are your in-laws this goes double. Arise at a reasonable hour, pitch in, and leave your bedroom and bathroom cleaner than when you arrived.

If you've been included in someone's holiday, be sure to call the person who hosted you and invite him later to one of your holidays, even if you think he will never come. Your host may always be hosting and truly relish being a guest for once.

MEDWAY SWEET POTATOES

There will be no arguing in your house when you adopt Gertrude Legendre's
tradition of serving these sweet potatoes for Thanksgiving and Christmas.
For more than sixty years, this esteemed doyenne owned and ran Medway
Plantation outside Charleston. She hosted lunch and dinner parties every
single day. Of course the fact that she had in-house staff of twenty went a
long way to bolstering her stamina. No gatherings were more anticipated
than Thanksgiving and Christmas and neither would have been as satisfying
if Medway Sweet Potatoes had not been served. The potatoes are light and
fluffy, with a crunchy sweet topping. There really is nothing not to love. The
memory of all other sweet potatoes will fade into oblivion. *SERVES 6 TO 8*

POTATOES
3 cups skinned, cooked (boiled
   or roasted), mashed sweet
   potatoes
½ cup sugar
½ cup whole milk
2 eggs, beaten
4 tablespoons butter, melted

1½ teaspoons pure vanilla extract
½ teaspoon salt

TOPPING
1 cup chopped pecans
½ cup brown sugar
⅓ cup flour
3 tablespoons butter, melted

Preheat the oven to 350°F.

MAKE THE POTATOES: In a large
bowl, mix together all the ingredients,
except for the topping. Spoon into a
1½-quart baking dish.

MAKE THE TOPPING: In a medium
bowl, stir together all the ingredients.
Spread the topping over the sweet
potatoes.

Bake in the oven for 35 minutes.
Serve immediately.

OVERNIGHT STAYS:

The Helpful Houseguest

If you did not grow up in a house with guests, how would you have ever learned how to be a houseguest? Visiting must not become a lost art! Let the Deans light the way.

There are different reasons why you stay at someone's house: You're passing through town and need a place to stay, you're visiting relatives, you're invited to a house party, or maybe you're going to help a friend in need. Believe it or not, the rules are different depending on what kind of guest you are.

THE NEED-A-PLACE TO STAY GUEST

If you are begging for a room in a major city, it is not lost on anyone that you are trying to save some money. You are not the first person to think longingly of your host's capacious guest room with you in it, leaving you free to spend your "savings" on gifts for your children, restaurants, or a rainy day. Your appreciation needs to be in proportion to what you are asking. It is your job to tread lightly and leave a pleasant experience in your wake.

First, state your purpose for coming—your niece's graduation, your job interview, whatever—so that your hosts will know you are not planning to be entertained by them. Check with them about their schedule as well, and pick a mutual time when you can do something together. Now is an excellent time to follow your instincts. Would your host like to have dinner cooked for them for a change? Maybe they'd simply enjoy a specialty cocktail made by you for them and taken into the den. Do something that expresses real gratitude.

If your host takes you up on dinner, just be sure you don't stick them with the bill or a mess. You need to do the shopping, cooking, and cleaning. For two to four people this is not difficult. Of course, no one expects you to cater a dinner for eight just because you are a houseguest.

We usually have no interest whatsoever in discussing food allergies and other dietary parameters. However, if you are making a thank-you meal for your hosts, be sure to determine what they can't eat and what they like to eat. No point in making a delicious gumbo if the people you're making it for cannot eat shellfish.

THE HOUSE-PARTY GUEST

House parties create a forced intimacy, so rare today, and will forge relationships and strengthen bonds in business, love, and every other aspect of your life. The Deans adore house parties and, of course, we know the ins and outs of what to do and why to do it. Multiple couples and families all meeting at one destination for several days creates a union that instantly infuses the occasion with giddy fun and expectation. It's akin to being back in a dorm.

Your host will have gone to considerably more trouble than when you've popped in for an overnight, so it's your job to be appreciative. You don't necessarily have to attend every activity on offer, but use your common sense. If great planning has been gone to—such as chartering a fishing boat, organizing a round-robin doubles tennis tournament, setting up a tour of a nearby attraction—you must participate. Plus, you don't want everyone discussing how churlish you are in your absence if you opt to nap instead.

Sometimes you will be invited to a country setting. Long leisurely walks, shooting skeet or game—these pursuits define house parties in South Carolina. If you're in a remote area, leaving may be difficult, but you may want to explore the surrounding area. Rent your own car and use the daytime hours to sightsee.

The glue to all house parties is the communal dinner where everyone cooks and gathers to relate the tales of the day. Some people have shopped, some have hiked, some have read, but everyone comes to dinner ready to report and celebrate as a group. Dinner attendance is mandatory.

"Who among us doesn't love a meatball?"

BRAISED LAMB MEATBALLS

Who among us doesn't love a meatball? If the alacrity with which lamb meatballs are snapped up at our events is any indication—everyone loves meatballs! The Deans' go-to meatballs are oven-baked in tomato sauce instead of fried, so our stovetops remain clean and our stomachs remain flat. Meatballs are great house-party food because everyone can participate in making them. Set up stations for the different tasks required. Many hands make light work.

There are many ways to serve these: drained from the tomato sauce and served with toothpicks, atop orzo pasta, with slices of warm pita bread, next to crisp oven-roasted potatoes—or best of all, nestled in the Academy's Southern Biscuit (see page 21) for sliders.

Lamb meatballs make great leftovers. Remember to always cool and reheat them in their braising liquid.

If you want to play with the flavors, here are some combinations we have enjoyed:

- Onion, garlic, basil, thyme
- Saffron, caramelized shallot
- Green olive, garlic, lemon zest
- Lime leaf, lemongrass, sambal oelek (Indonesian chili paste)
- Ginger, orange zest, gochujang (Korean chili paste)

SERVES 6 TO 8

½ cup whole milk

1¼ cups day-old sourdough bread crumbs (pea-size pieces), lightly toasted

½ teaspoon cumin seeds

½ teaspoon coriander seeds

½ teaspoon fennel pollen or toasted ground fennel seeds

1 small onion, finely diced

3 tablespoons olive oil

3 cloves garlic, finely chopped

2 pounds ground lamb (preferably 85% lean)

¼ cup finely chopped fresh parsley

¼ teaspoon smoked paprika

½ teaspoon piment D'Espelette (dried Basque chile) or New Mexican red chile powder

Sea salt and freshly cracked black pepper

Seasoned crushed canned plum tomatoes, preferably San Marzano, for covering the meatballs

In a bowl, pour the milk over the bread crumbs to soak.

In a small, dry skillet, toast the cumin and coriander seeds (and also fennel seeds, if using instead of pollen) over medium heat until fragrant. Let cool, then grind in a spice grinder or mortar and pestle.

In a large, heavy skillet, sauté the onion in 1 tablespoon of the olive oil over medium-low heat, stirring often, until medium brown. Add the garlic (adding the garlic too soon will burn the garlic before the onions are ready). Let cool and reserve.

In a large bowl, combine the ground lamb, soaked bread crumbs, onion-garlic mixture, toasted spices, fennel pollen (if using), parsley, paprika, and piment d'Espelette; season with salt and pepper. Mix thoroughly but gently with your hands (overworking the meatballs will adversely affect the texture and make hard little meatballs). Refrigerate for at least 1 hour.

Preheat the oven to 475°F. Line a heavy baking sheet with foil and coat with 1 tablespoon of the oil. Gently form the meat into 1½-inch meatballs and place them on the foil-lined sheet. Brush with the remaining 1 tablespoon olive oil. Roast until well browned, 14 to 18 minutes.

Reduce the oven temperature to 275°F. Gently transfer the meatballs to a baking dish and add enough crushed tomatoes to cover (it is important to cover the meatballs completely so that they finish cooking in a wet environment). Bake for 30 minutes.

ROAST PORK IN A SKILLET

Americans love a one-pot meal—one pot, one mess. Here's our favorite pork-and-greens version. You can take it one step further and top with cooked root vegetables, such as beets, or roasted apples. *SERVES 4*

4-rib pork loin, with generous
    fat cap
Salt
1 loaf sourdough bread, crusts
    trimmed and bread cut into

1-inch cubes
Dark greens, such as Swiss chard,
    mustard greens, or escarole,
    washed and torn

One hour before cooking, rub the pork top and bottom with lots of salt. This is a dry brine, so be generous with the salt.

Preheat the oven to 400°F. Place the pork loin in a cast-iron skillet and roast for 1 hour five minutes. Remove from the oven and transfer to a serving platter. After its gauntlet in the oven, the loin is exhausted, so let it rest for 15 minutes.

Pour off some of the fat from the skillet. Toss the sourdough croutons into the skillet, along with a handful of greens. Roast in the oven during the loin's nap and toss every five minutes.

Slice the loin and serve with the vegetables and croutons.

BREAKFASTS TO BOND OVER

We all know dinner is fun with all the wine and cocktails flowing and the subsequent revelry, but you might be surprised to find that breakfast can be even more fun. You will rehash last night's events and make new plans for the day, so the meal is suspended between past and future. Nowadays, an enormous breakfast is almost extinct, but why? Aren't some of our most favorite foods breakfast foods: sticky buns, extra-crisp bacon, blueberry pancakes, coffee? Even vegetarians are put in a better mood by the aroma of frying bacon and the sight of scrambled eggs, whether they want to eat them or not. The breakfast alone is enough of a reason to plan a house party.

———— c ————

EGG STRATA

To the classic recipe here, try adding sautéed or grilled mushrooms, onions, spinach, asparagus, or tomatoes (layer them in the pan just before you pour in the eggs). Assemble the strata in time for it to be refrigerated overnight before baking. *SERVES 6*

1 sourdough boule, sliced ¾ inch
   thick
6 tablespoons unsalted butter
Thin slices of Gruyère or cheddar,
   enough to cover the bread on
   the bottom of the pan

6 eggs
3 cups whole milk
1 pound bulk sausage, browned

Grease a 9-by-11-inch glass or ceramic baking dish. Spread both sides of the bread with the butter. Layer the bread in the bottom of the baking dish. Top with the cheese.

In a medium bowl, whisk together the eggs and milk. Pour over the bread, up to a ½ inch below the top of the baking dish. Any more liquid will bubble over when cooking. Add the sausage. Cover and refrigerate the strata overnight or for up to 2 days.

Preheat the oven to 375°F. Bake the strata until puffy and golden brown, 45 minutes to 1 hour.

HASH BROWNS IN DUCK FAT & CREAM

The only problem with offering this decadent hash to guests is that they will never want to leave your house (check our manners section, page 193, on best guest-removal practices). Serving this hash will make you and your guests feel like the most cosseted and loved people in the world. You, because it is deceptively easy to create, and your guests, because it tastes too good to be true.

Cooking potatoes in duck fat is awesome, which is why both Deans keep tubs of duck fat in our freezers at all times. This recipe cooks the potatoes in two stages, just like classic pomme frites. The potatoes will have a light fluffy interior contrasted with a shatteringly crisp exterior. The price of the duck fat, available at gourmet markets, might seem exorbitant, but as long as it is not scorched and is strained before storing in a tightly covered container in your freezer, it can be reused up to six times. Duck fat will soon become a go-to ingredient in your kitchen. *SERVES 6*

2 pounds baking potatoes, peeled and cut into ⅔-inch cubes

2 pounds duck fat

3 shallots, thinly sliced

¼ cup dry sherry

1 cup heavy cream

½ teaspoon freshly cracked black pepper

2 tablespoons chives, snipped

1 tablespoon finely chopped fresh tarragon

1 tablespoon chopped fresh parsley

Sea salt

Rinse the potatoes in cold water until the water runs clear. This removes the excess starch and will allow you to get a crisp exterior.

In a large pot, heat the duck fat to 320°F on a deep-fat thermometer. Add the potatoes and fry until fully cooked through—test with a toothpick, cake tester, or paring knife to see if they are soft in the middle. Drain and let cool.

Increase the heat of the duck fat until the temperature reaches 360°F. Return the potatoes to the pan and fry until deep golden brown and crisp, 4 to 6 minutes. Remove from the heat and transfer to a paper-towel-lined baking sheet to cool.

In another skillet, cook the shallots in 1 tablespoon duck fat over medium-high heat until softened and browned, about 5 minutes. Add the sherry and cook until the pan is almost dry. Add the cream and black pepper and cook until reduced by two thirds.

Add the crisp potatoes, chives, tarragon, and parsley. Toss, season with salt, and serve immediately.

SERVING OPTION: *Dice some smoked ham or shredded duck confit (or caramelized onions and roasted mushrooms) and stir into the potatoes. Spoon into six ramekins, crack an egg on each ramekin, and put on a sheet pan or large baking dish. Slide into a 350°F oven for about 4 minutes.*

ENGLISH MUFFINS

Why are homemade English muffins necessary to your life? Because eaten for breakfast, slathered in melted butter and honey, they are sublime. Have you ever put your grilled hamburger on one? Beyond good. If you go to the trouble to make these yourself you must fork-split them, which means going around the circumference of the muffin plunging the tines of a fork towards the center until the muffin breaks open. The irregularity of the cut is what creates all the famous nooks and crannies for capturing precious juices.

MAKES 8 TO 10 MUFFINS

¾ cup buttermilk

1 tablespoon sugar

1 package active dry yeast
(do not use quick action)

½ cup warm water

3 tablespoons butter, melted and
cooled

1½ teaspoons coarse sea salt

3 cups unbleached all-purpose
flour

Cornmeal, for sprinkling

Warm the buttermilk in a small saucepan, then remove from the heat. Mix in the sugar until it dissolves. Let cool. In a small bowl, dissolve the yeast in the warm water. Let stand until bubbly and creamy, about 10 minutes.

In a large bowl, combine the warm buttermilk, yeast mixture, butter, and salt. Stir in 2 cups of the flour with a wooden spoon and beat until smooth (alternatively, beat in a standing mixer). Continue adding the flour, ½ cup at a time, to make a smooth, soft dough that is just slightly sticky. Knead the dough for a minute. Place in a greased bowl, cover, and let rise until doubled in bulk, about 1 hour. A chilled dough is easier to handle. Alternatively, cover and let rise in the refrigerator overnight.

Punch down the dough. Using a pastry cutter or knife, divide the dough into 8 or 10 pieces; roll into balls. Sprinkle a baking sheet with cornmeal. Set the dough balls on the pan and press each round with the heel of your hand to slightly flatten. Flip the rounds over so each side has a bit of cornmeal sticking to the dough. Cover with a clean dish towel and let rise for 30 minutes. Muffins can be covered with plastic wrap and refrigerated for up to 3 days.

Preheat oven to 250°F. Heat a large skillet over medium-low heat. Add the dough rounds and cook slowly until lightly browned, turning once, about 20 minutes. When the muffins are finished cooking in the frying pans, with a spatula, place them back on their baking sheets. Bake for another 10 minutes to finish cooking. Let cool. (The muffins will keep in an airtight container for 3 days or frozen for up to 1 month.)

To serve, split the muffins with a fork and toast both sides.

A FRIEND IN NEED

Being a houseguest is sometimes about bringing equilibrium back into a house, whether around a celebratory occasion, like your daughter having a baby, or a somber one, like your best friend receiving chemotherapy. When life throws us major shifts and shocks, the routine of domesticity is most crucial, but it's also barely attainable. Now is the time for you to step in and use your skills to run someone else's house. Even if the recipients are barely able to eat or join in the conversation, having daily life going on around them proclaims, "There will be a way through this situation." Everyone is buoyed by extra love—including you, the giver of kindness to someone in need.

Be sensitive about your length of stay, but be overly generous with your provisions. Good cheer and delicious food (including a freezerful when you leave, even if unmentioned at the time), will be remembered for a lifetime.

———— ✿ ————

CHICKEN PIE

When brought to one's knees by life's vicissitudes, your body and soul crave comfort. We've gone around and around Robin Hood's barn and it's simple: Chicken pie is the ultimate comfort food. It's delicious and soothing, pastry and protein, Southern and Northern—what more could you ask of a recipe? Of course the Deans couldn't help putting a few riffs on the classic. *SERVES 6*

3½ pounds skinless, boneless chicken thighs

1 pound wild mushrooms or 2½ ounces dried wild mushrooms

2 cups chicken stock

2 to 3 tablespoons butter

1 large onion, chopped

2 carrots, halved lengthwise and cut crosswise ¼ inch thick

1 cup fresh or frozen peas

1 tablespoon unbleached all-purpose flour

1 cup heavy cream

½ cup dry sherry

1 tablespoon chopped fresh flat-leaf parsley

1 tablespoon chopped fresh thyme

Salt and freshly ground black pepper

Potpie Pastry, rolled out (see page 173)

1 egg white, beaten

In a large saucepan, simmer the chicken thighs in water to cover until almost cooked through, about 20 minutes. Let cool, then pull into large pieces.

If using dried mushrooms, place in a bowl and cover with boiling water; let soak for 30 minutes. Strain the mushroom liquid through a piece of doubled cheesecloth to avoid grit, reserving the mushroom stock. Do not waste this mushroom elixir. Measure the mushroom stock and add enough chicken stock to make up 2 cups. In a medium saucepan, bring the 2 cups chicken stock (or mushroom-chicken stock) to a boil and cook until reduced to 1 cup.

In a large skillet, melt 2 tablespoons butter until foaming. Add the onion, carrots, and peas (if using fresh) and sauté over medium-low heat. Cover the vegetables and sweat until the onion is softened, about 10 minutes. In a large saucepan, sauté the fresh mushrooms (if using) in 1 tablespoon butter, until the mushrooms have released all of their liquid and browned slightly. Add to the other vegetables.

Add the flour to the vegetables and cook until evenly coated. Slowly stir in the reduced stock and bring to a simmer, until the mixture begins to thicken, about 5 minutes. Stir in the cream and sherry, then fold in the parsley and thyme. Return to a gentle simmer and cook for 5 minutes. Add the chicken and frozen peas (if using); season with salt and pepper. (The mixture can be refrigerated at this point for up to 24 hours.) Divide the chicken mixture among four ramekins or spread in one large baking dish.

Preheat the oven to 375°F. If using individual ramekins, cut out 4 disks of the Potpie Pastry, using an overturned ramekin as your guide; place one disk on top of each ramekin. If using a single baking dish, flip the silicone sheet of Potpie Pastry onto the baking dish; remove the silicone sheet. Press the pastry slightly to the baking dish(es) to adhere. Brush the top of the pastry with the egg white.

Bake the pie(s) for 45 minutes. Let cool slightly.

POTPIE PASTRY

1½ cups all-purpose flour

1½ teaspoons baking powder

1 teaspoon salt

3 tablespoons butter

3 ounces goat cheese, crumbled

¾ to 1 cup plain whole-milk
  yogurt

1 teaspoon fresh thyme
  (optional)

freshly ground black pepper

In a large bowl, combine the flour, baking power, and salt. Cut in the butter with a pastry blender or two knives, until the butter is the size of small peas. Add the cheese and toss until blended. Stir in the yogurt, thyme, and pepper until the mixture comes together.

Place the dough on a silicone baking sheet or floured surface, dust the top with extra flour, and roll out with a rolling pin. Fold one side of the dough into the middle and then the other and roll out again to ¼ inch thick.

RUM POUND CAKE

If there is to be only one cake in your arsenal, then the Deans suggest a pound cake. These cakes are delicious plain, but they also like being glazed, getting sliced and toasted, and, of course, playing with whipped cream, because who doesn't?

For pound cakes, the Deans have banished Bundt pans from the halls of the Academy. We hear your collective sharp intake of breath, but do not be addled. After baking 1,500 pound cakes, we know of what we speak. First, the ridges and peaks in a Bundt pan are time-consuming and annoying to butter and flour. Second, and much more important, in dislodging your masterpiece, you invert the cake so that its crisp, golden crust sits on the bottom. We prefer a ten-inch tube pan instead. A tube pan is flat, it is easily greased and floured, and once the cake has been removed from the pan, you can invert the cake upright to show off its gorgeous top, as it should be. Pound cake is thusly named because originally they were created with one pound flour, one pound butter, one pound sugar, and one pound of eggs. The recipe has been refined over the ages.

3½ cups flour

½ teaspoon salt

½ teaspoon baking powder

⅓ cup rum or bourbon

1 vanilla bean, seeds scraped

3 sticks (12 ounces) unsalted
butter, at room temperature

3 cups sugar

8 eggs, at room temperature

1 cup sour cream

Lemon, Rum, or Bourbon Glaze, if
desired (recipe follows)

Preheat the oven to 325°F. Butter and flour a 10-inch tube pan (or spray with cooking spray). In a large bowl, combine the flour, salt, and baking powder. In a small bowl, combine the rum and vanilla seeds.

Using an electric mixer, beat the butter on medium speed until creamy. Add the sugar slowly, and continue mixing on medium-high speed until light and fluffy, about 8 minutes. Scrape down the bowl several times.

Add the eggs 1 at a time to the butter mixture, scraping down the bowl and beater. The batter will be a little lumpy. Add the flour mixture in two parts alternately with the rum mixture in two parts, beating just to incorporate. Stir in the sour cream. Spoon the batter into the prepared pan. Bake the cake until a toothpick inserted in the center comes out clean, 1½ hours. Turn the oven off and let the cake cool in the oven for 15 minutes, then remove. If using the glaze, drizzle it over the top of the cake while the cake is still warm. Let the cake cool and the glaze set before slicing. Both Deans agree that cakes must never be refrigerated, so be patient. We keep our cakes on the counter under a cake dome, and you should as well.

LEMON, RUM, OR BOURBON GLAZE

Glazes are delicious, easy to make, and won't go unnoticed. Incredibly, we are giving you three glazes for the price of this one book. To make 1 cup of glaze, in a small saucepan, combine 1½ cups sugar and one of the following flavors: ¼ cup fresh lemon juice, rum, or bourbon; and ½ teaspoon pure vanilla extract. Cook over low heat, whisking constantly, until the sugar dissolves. Use warm.

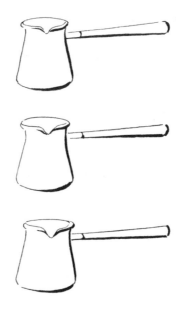

"Three glazes for the price of this one book."

THE REINVITED GUEST

As a guest, you enjoy your host's company and vice versa, but there can be too much of a good thing. Your presence, de facto, means that your host has changed his daily routine, so you must be sensitive to the fact that you are altering someone's schedule.

Let's run through a day of being a houseguest:

> **MORNING** – If you arise earlier than your host, you need to be in charge of your own coffee. The night before, locate the coffee and all its accoutrements. If your host receives a newspaper, he probably has a daily ritual with that paper, which does not include you. Do your news reading online, bring a book, or go take a walk, being sure to leave a note to indicate when you'll return.

> **AFTERNOON** – If you have been out with your host all afternoon, when you come home, absent yourself for an hour or two at least. Self-sufficiency is the catchword of a smart houseguest. Always leave your host wanting more of you (you never want anyone to count down the minutes until you leave). Here's a useful tip: Always slip off your high heels, so you don't make too much noise clacking around the house.

> **EVENING** – You can help with a dinner plan. Did you pick a restaurant or make the reservation? If staying home, why don't you set the table or take charge of cocktails? Pay attention. If your host seems to have dinner under control and cooking relaxes him, don't keep asking what you can do to help. If preparing the meal looks like it is a chore, take charge of certain tasks.

NIGHT – What about after dinner? Usually the first night of your stay is the most revelatory and everyone may want to stay up late. By night two or three, unless you are staying with a real party cat, beg off around nine o'clock, so you can all enjoy a little time alone. If you want to check out nightlife, reenter the house on little cat feet. Remember all those nights you snuck out as a teenager? Repurpose those skills to sneak back in.

DEPARTURE – Ask before you strip the bed—don't assume that this is a wanted task. If you have not seen, and there has been no reference to a housecleaner, don't assume one is coming to mop up after you. Wipe down the bathroom and take your towels to the washing machine.

AFTER YOU LEAVE – A handwritten thank-you note is best, but the Deans can see that the Internet is here to stay, so we can no longer be miffed if we receive an e-mail instead (especially since we seem to do it ourselves).

HOSTESS GIFTS

Hostess gifts are a real dilemma. Very few people have mastered what to give, which is why regifting is so popular. Regifting—it's not the worst thing in the world. The gift might not suit you completely but a friend might like it. But re-gifters beware: Make sure there is no gift card addressed to you inside the box.

Here are a few general hostess-gift suggestions that will keep you on track:

WHEN YOU ARRIVE...

One bottle of wine smacks of a regift. Two of the same kind, or an interesting pairing of white and red do not.

If you are going in the direction of a scented candle, tread carefully. Many scents can be off-putting. For some sophisticated ideas, try the candles from Taffin and Diptyque.

A pound of the house-brand coffee from a special coffee house (not a chain), with a scoop attached, will please all coffee drinkers (and non-coffee drinkers can easily regift this one).

Cut flowers are problematic for a dinner party, because a vase has to be procured at the last minute. However, a person can never have too many orchids (if you gave a cocktail party for one hundred and everyone brought an orchid, wouldn't you instantly decide to make that party an annual event?).

A cheese board with a selection of unusual cheeses and crackers is a great gift.

Any homemade food is appreciated. If you arrive bearing cookies, fudge, English muffins, refrigerator jams, pickles, chutneys, and so on, your thoughtfulness and effort will be noticed.

AFTER YOU LEAVE...

A photo album, drawings, pressed leaves and flowers—these personalize the weekend you spent together.

Depending on the size of the house party, guests will go through a case of wine in the course of the weekend. A replacement case after you've gone is always welcome.

Make a donation to your host's favorite charity in his name.

Give a gift certificate to a local restaurant, butcher shop, beauty shop, or spa.

REFRIGERATOR WATERMELON RIND PICKLES

The shiny green orb with its hot pink center beckons you from the produce department. Once all the flesh has been devoured, we throw away the rind. Or, do we? The Deans don't. We pickle the rind into strips of unsurpassed succulence. Lines form outside the Academy when people realize it's watermelon rind pickling day. Children and elderly alike elbow one another jockeying for position, lest we run out before they get a piece. *MAKES 4 PINTS*

Rind from 1 medium watermelon with a little of the pink watermelon flesh remaining, cut into 1-by-1½-inch pieces
1 cup kosher salt

1 quart apple cider vinegar
4 cups sugar
4 cinnamon sticks
2 to 4 jalapeños, thinly sliced

In a large bowl, layer the rind and salt, alternating the two. Cover with cold water; cover the bowl and refrigerate overnight. Place the rind in a colander and rinse with cool tap water several times, tossing the rinds with your hands.

In a large saucepan, bring the cider vinegar, sugar, and cinnamon sticks to a simmer over medium heat.

Cook, stirring, until all the sugar has dissolved. Add the watermelon rind and jalapeños and boil gently, stirring occasionally, until the watermelon is translucent, about 1 hour.

Place the mixture in sterile mason jars and seal tightly with new lids. The pickled watermelon rinds will keep in the refrigerator for 3 months.

PEACH GINGER CHUTNEY

Just saying the word *chutney* conjures up images of Indian palaces and rajas in gorgeous silks riding around on elephants. Silver platters mounded with rice and the most fiery curries are tempered by what? That's right. Chutney! But its use shouldn't be limited to Far Eastern travel. It can be paired with hot dogs on the Fourth of July, or with grilled chicken and roast pork for exalted dinners. Amaze your friends and family with your sophistication. The Deans will keep it a secret that you learned it here. *MAKES FOUR 8-OUNCE JARS*

10 whole black peppercorns

1 tablespoon mustard seeds

¼ cup grated grapefruit peel

⅔ cup freshly squeezed grapefruit juice

6 cups chopped, peeled peaches

5 cups light brown sugar

3½ cups cider vinegar

3 cups chopped onions

1½ cups coarsely chopped dried
   apricots

2 tablespoons finely chopped
   garlic

3 tablespoons finely chopped
   fresh ginger

1 tablespoon curry powder

1 teaspoon allspice

Tie peppercorns and mustard seeds in a piece of cheesecloth, making a spice bag.

In a large saucepan combine the grapefruit peel and juice, peaches, brown sugar, vinegar, onions, apricots, garlic, and ginger. Bring to a boil over medium-high heat, stirring occasionally. Reduce heat and simmer for 1 hour, stirring occasionally. Add the curry, allspice, and the spice bag, and simmer for 30 minutes more, until thick enough to stay on a spoon. Discard the spice bag.

Meanwhile, put jars and lids into a stock pot, covered with water. Bring to a boil, turn off, and let sit until ready to fill.

Ladle hot chutney into the clean, hot jars, leaving ¼ inch of headspace. Screw on the tops. Refrigerate for up to 3 months.

PIERRE'S PEPPERY PICKLES

One of the main reasons Dean Manigault married Pierre is because he had this pickle recipe. Once she discovered how easy they were, however, she promptly got a divorce and now she makes them herself.

If you can boil and measure, and not even at the same time, refrigerator pickles are well within your reach. All the fear of heat processing and sterilizing is removed from pickle making. You simply concoct a brine of your choosing, pour it over the cucumbers or other vegetables to be pickled, and refrigerate. Some take a week or two to cure, but after that it's crunch time! These will keep in the refrigerator for up to 3 months, but the Deans are here to tell you that ours never last that long. *MAKES FOUR 8-OUNCE JARS*

6 cups sliced pickling cucumbers (Kirby)

1 onion, peeled and sliced ¼-inch thick

3 cups cider vinegar

1 cup sugar

2 tablespoons pickling, canning or kosher salt

1 tablespoon prepared white horseradish (the Deans recommend buying the horseradish in the refrigerator section as opposed to the room temperature bottles on the shelf)

2 teaspoons celery seeds

2 teaspoons dry mustard

1 teaspoon ground turmeric

In a bowl, combine the cucumbers and onion.

In a saucepan over medium-high heat, combine the vinegar, sugar, salt, horseradish, celery seeds, dry mustard, and turmeric. Bring to a boil. Reduce the heat and boil gently for 3 minutes. Allow the mixture to cool (for maximum crispness in your pickles).

Pack the cucumbers and onions into jars. Ladle pickling liquid into jars, leaving ¼ inch of headspace at the top of the jar. Screw on the lids.

Refrigerate for at least 1 day. For more intense results refrigerate for up to 2 weeks, but you may not be able to wait this long. Use within 3 months.

PETS AND CHILDREN

Nobody really wants pets or children as houseguests, though no host is actually going to tell you that. This is true even for people who *adore* dogs—they do not want yours in their house. You never want to arrive for a visit looking like the *Grapes of Wrath*'s Joads crossing the country, with granny on the roof in her rocker, your grimy children, the dog, and all your possessions stuffed in a suitcase. When traveling by yourself you are light and unencumbered.

"Nobody really wants pets or children as houseguests."

Transform Your Dining Table
Into an ATM Machine

"To Churchill, meals weren't just a matter of getting something to eat. They were social occasions, which he used to cement alliances and sway opponents, to elicit information, and to shine.... Churchill's table-top diplomacy, his use of dinner parties and meals to accomplish what he believed could not always be accomplished in the more formal setting of a conference room."

BOOKSHELF BY HENRIK BERING,
WALL STREET JOURNAL, JAN 15, 2013

The Deans have used meals at their dining room tables as opportunities for everything from asking a favor, to getting an interview, to securing a book deal, closing a sale, and even starting a relationship. We've practically turned our dining room tables into ATM machines spewing money. On none of these occasions did the Deans start hammering away at the person, now trapped in our house, to get results for us immediately. We are far more subtle than that. Before we go in for the kill, we feed you. You sit around a well-set table, basking in the glow of candlelight and conversation, enjoying sumptuous home-cooked food, and before you know it, you are ready to say yes, and you don't even know what the ask is.

Of course, it's not quite as simple as we make it sound. The key to success lies in exhibiting no ostentation, either in food or dress. Lobster and low-cut tops scream, "love me love me" and distort your message. You want the entire evening to be remembered, not any one aspect highlighted above

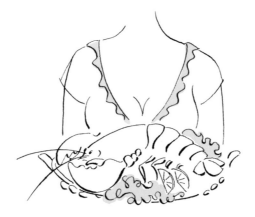

the others. The first step is mastering a meal that is delicious, simple, and accessible to all palates. The next step is gathering the right group to support your cause—it could be one extra person, or four or five. Do not divulge your mission to anyone, because you do not want any guest inadvertently throwing the mission off course.

Wenda Millard, business woman par excellence, did not become synonymous with swanky dinner parties by mismanaging her dining room. When entertaining business associates, she has a sixth sense for a harassing, unwarranted sales pitch. She immediately interrupts and steers the conversation to smoother topics.

The table should be bathed in candlelight so everyone looks their best. You need to have everything in a total state of preparedness when your guests walk in the door: the table set, the chicken roasted, and you dressed and scented. Your obvious command over the evening puts everyone at ease instantly.

A simple meal leaves much less opportunity for mistakes. Remember, you and your table are working together tonight. You are highlighting your competency while the table is creating the intimacy. Your stage has been set.

"Powerful people are at their most vulnerable first thing in the morning."

Pay attention to your intuition. The three tenets to insure a successful business evening are:

HAVE A SCHEDULE, casually share it with your guests, and stick to it. Everyone gets nervous if the end of the evening is not in sight, especially people who do not know you well.

MAKE SURE your business associate's spouse has a fabulous time. When they go home, that person becomes your PR representative.

DON'T GET DRUNK. If you don't know why, the Deans cannot help you.

Business meals don't have to be just dinners. Think outside the entertaining box. Some of the Deans' most fruitful work relationships began over breakfast in our own kitchens. Who wouldn't admire a person who hands them the best stack of pancakes they ever tasted? Homemade sticky buns and fresh coffee in your house is a better experience than Starbucks could ever be. If you want to get real business done with a powerful person, invite them over for breakfast. A morning meal does not interrupt anyone's day and the Deans have learned that powerful people are at their most vulnerable first thing in the morning. It is necessary, however, for your partner to be in attendance so as not to give the wrong impression as to your intention.

Sometimes luncheons around our dining room tables are the most productive. The Academy dining tables work overtime during the weekdays. We frequently host business luncheons at the Academy and we consider this the most elegant form of multitasking.

Clubbing with Your Besties

———— ⁃ ————

Supper clubs
Bridge clubs
Book clubs
Discussion clubs
Birthday clubs

What we like about clubs is that they group people together in clusters that wouldn't necessarily form by themselves. The glue of the group is the common interest. After several meetings, you will be surprised at the intimacy that is formed and the new friends you have. A good bridge player or an English teacher might not be among your closest friends right now, but if you join a club with them, over the course of a year, maybe they will be.

THE SUPPER CLUB

If there is a group of people you want to see on a regular basis, the supper club is a good way to force everyone to put the date on their calendars and make sure the event takes place. What this event lacks in spontaneity it makes up for in stolidity. Arranging time with friends can be difficult, and we champion any activity that lures people out of cyberspace and into face time. We advocate a private house over a restaurant, always. Pick four to six couples and three or four dates a year, and rotate the event among your houses. Voilà! You have a supper club.

THE BRIDGE CLUB

The Deans have never been to a bridge club. Perhaps our not knowing how to play bridge holds us back, but maybe we are just imaging things. If we did play bridge, we would have formed a bridge club long ago and set ourselves to hosting subsequent parties, because they sound so old-fashioned

"Perhaps our not knowing how to play bridge holds us back."

and sophisticated. When we imagine bridge clubs, we picture dainty tea sandwiches, one strong cocktail, and enough gossip to keep us in the know. In fact, the thought of this much elegance might even spur us on to start taking bridge lessons immediately.

THE BOOK CLUB

The Deans have been in many book clubs and mark our words: There are dangers in these here waters. Our genius lies in the domestic arts, not literary criticism. When we go to a book club, we like to hear an authority in literature hold forth. The most successful book clubs are anchored by a mental heavyweight. This scholar should lead the discussion and be given free rein to cut off annoying speeches. We notice that the very people who have the least to say are frequently the ones who speak the most often and for the longest. What we do like about book clubs is they force us to read tomes we would not have chosen for ourselves and to visit with people who are outside our usual circle of friends.

THE DISCUSSION CLUB

A discussion club is akin to a twentieth-century Parisian salon. Pick a subject that you are passionate about, look around your community, and invite people who you think might be similarly interested. The difficulty is to pick a weighty enough topic to hold everyone's interest for an hour or more. To prevent your salon from turning into a cocktail party, discourage the inclusion of spouses. Everyone must commit to at least five meetings to ascertain if the group can really gel.

THE BIRTHDAY CLUB

We know of a group of ladies whose husbands tend to forget their birthdays. As sensible women, they have formed a club to celebrate their birthdays together and leave their husbands to wonder where they went. Every two months, they band together and the two people with the closest birthday do not pay for or cook dinner. A big shout-out from the Deans to these resourceful, smart, plucky ladies!

TEA SANDWICHES FOR CLUBS

Pepperidge Farm sells very thin white and wheat breads. They must have started in the tea-sandwich business, so perfect are these breads for that purpose. To ensure the bread does not get too soggy when making tomato and cucumber sandwiches, place your paper-thin disks of vegetables on a piece of paper towel and sprinkle lightly with salt. Allow them to weep gently into the paper towel while you the butter the bread and trim the crusts. After a good cry, the vegetables will not slime up your sandwiches.

HORS D'OEUVRES MENU FOR CLUBS

If your club begins at five or six o'clock, cocktails and hors d'oeuvres are warranted. Artfully arrange a large platter of delectables that can be picked up by the fingers: dried apricots, olives, pickled beets, pistachios, slices of coppa and salami, a delicious cheese cut into small pieces, a spreadable cheese on toasts and crackers, etc. Aim for a variety of colors, textures, and flavors. You've created a bazaar right on your table. Everyone will find something they like.

DESSERT MENU FOR CLUBS

You won't disappoint if you just serve desserts at one of your meetings, depending on the time of the get-together. If it's at an in-between-meals hour or late night, an all-sweets menu is a fun departure from the usual savory nibbles. The choices can be an assortment of homemade cookies in the shapes of hearts, clubs, spades, and diamonds, or a singular, spectacular ginger cheesecake, or a pairing of boozy hot chocolate and biscotti.

"Serve only one per guest, even if they beg for more."

BOOZY HOT CHOCOLATE

This is not a dessert drink for the faint of heart. This hot cocoa is deceptively strong and meant to be served in an oversized latte cup. Serve only one per guest, even if they beg for more. As the recipe calls for sugar-laden liquors and garnishes, it is important to use unsweetened cocoa powder. *MAKES 1 DRINK*

2 tablespoons high-quality unsweetened Dutch-process cocoa

1 cup whole milk

1 ounce (2 tablespoons) coffee liqueur, such as Kahlúa

1 ounce (2 tablespoons) almond liqueur, such as amaretto Disaronno

1 ounce (2 tablespoons) vanilla-flavored vodka, such as Stolichnaya Vanil

Garnishes: whipped cream, ice cream, frothed milk, marshmallows, shaved chocolate, ground toasted nuts

In a small, heavy saucepan, dissolve the cocoa in 3 tablespoons of the milk over low heat. Add the remaining milk, bring to a simmer, and then reduce the heat to very low. Add the liqueurs and vodka. Once steam starts to rise, pour into an oversize mug. Garnish to your preference.

GINGER CHEESECAKE

A spicy cheesecake for our spicy lady friends.

CRUST

1½ cups gingersnaps, crushed

6 tablespoons unsalted butter,
  melted

¼ cup granulated sugar

FILLING

2 pounds cream cheese, softened

½ cup sugar

½ cup brown sugar

4 large eggs, at room temperature,
  lightly beaten

½ cup heavy cream

½ cup chopped candied ginger

2 tablespoons grated fresh ginger

1 teaspoon ground ginger

1 teaspoon pure vanilla extract

Preheat the oven to 300°F.

MAKE THE CRUST: In a medium bowl, combine the gingersnaps, butter, and sugar. Mix well. Press the mixture evenly on the bottom and partly up the sides of a 9-inch springform pan. Let chill in the freezer while you make the filling.

MAKE THE FILLING: Using a standing mixer, beat the cream cheese and sugars until light and smooth. Add the eggs and completely blend in. Then mix in the cream, all the gingers, and the vanilla. Pour the filling into the prepared pan.

Bake the cheesecake for 1 hour and 40 minutes. You will be able to tell if the cheesecake is done by looking at it—the top should look firm in the center and beginning to brown, the sides will be raised slightly. Turn off the oven and leave the cake in the oven for another hour with the door ajar (stick a wooden spoon in between the oven door and the oven). Remove from the oven and let cool on a rack to room temperature, then cover with plastic wrap and refrigerate for at least 6 hours before serving. The cheesecake is even tastier if it is allowed to chill overnight.

How to Comport Yourself

Etiquette is important because it saves people from offending other members of society. While the word *etiquette* may seem outdated, how could being offensive ever be in vogue?

Let's start at the table. Nothing turns the Deans off faster than poor table manners. If we see them, we turn to ice. Of course, we are always gracious, hospitable, and polite under any circumstances, but that doesn't mean we don't notice everything. We do. Below are the hard-and-fast rules as per the Deans:

- **NO ELBOWS ON THE TABLE**, sit up straight, and no slouching. These rules came to be so that conversation can be generated. If you are one inch off your plate shoveling food in your face as quickly as possible, you will never be able to utter one word. This is why teenagers are renowned for not being the finest conversationalists. Observe a cluster of them and notice the lack of distance between plate and face.

- **NEVER SWITCH PLACE CARDS.** This is the basest form of party sabotage! Even if you are seated between two absolute nightmares, get over yourself. The hostess will know you've switched cards and you will engender bad feelings. You've insulted the people you were supposed to sit next to, and you've shown yourself to be incredibly selfish. Yuck.

- **DON'T BURDEN YOUR HOSTS** with your food restrictions. If you have a life-threatening allergy, discreetly ask what's in the dish. Otherwise, no one wants to know the parameters of your diet. Simply don't eat what you can't and snack when you get home. This point is so vital that we have decided to stress it a second time.

IF YOU ARE SERVED TABLESIDE, there should be two utensils on the platter. Put one utensil under the food and secure the other one on top, and transfer the food to your plate. Do not serve the person next to you; they will be served in good time. Don't take too much food—when food is passed at a party it is usually passed twice, so you will have an opportunity to get seconds.

DO NOT BEGIN EATING UNTIL your hostess has had her first bite. If there are multiple tables in the room, you need not wait for your hostess, but you do need to wait for everyone at your table to be served.

DO NOT GRAB YOUR KNIFE or fork with your fist and start sawing your meat like you are cutting down a tree. Your left index finger should be on the back of the fork, right above the tines, and your right index finger on the back of the knife right above the blade. This affords maximum control and dexterity. Having severed a bite-size piece of food, simply raise the fork to your mouth with your left hand. Do not switch the fork to your right hand, an extra and unnerving step. The law applies to right- and left-handed people alike.

FOOD VISIBLE DURING mastication is a big problem. Do not speak to us until you have fully swallowed all items in your mouth. Seeing partially chewed food in your mouth makes us feel like we are eating with a wild animal. A cheetah in the Serengeti knows better.

* **CHEW QUIETLY.** You may have this problem and not even know it, because no one is brave enough tell you, so ask a trusted friend or relative.

* **WHEN TAKING BUTTER** off the butter plate, transfer it to your own plate before applying it to the bread. Why? We do not know, it's just the way it's done. Also, the bread should be in bite-size pieces. Please don't slather the whole slice and eat it like an open-faced sandwich.

* **LEAVE YOUR NAPKIN** on your chair seat if you get up from the table at any point. If you have been leaving your napkin on the table, you have been wrong. A soiled napkin is a wrinkled, stained reminder of previously eaten food, and no one wants to see it.

* **DO NOT LEAVE YOUR TEASPOON,** soup spoon, or coffee spoon in the cup or bowl. Retire it to the saucer or plate beneath instead. Your spoon should not be waving like a little flag telling everyone you don't know better.

* **YOU ARE IN CHARGE** of your own good time. When you accept an invitation you are signing an unwritten contract that you will be as charming and sociable as you know how to be. You are not doing your hosts any favor by arriving and sitting in the corner waiting to be entertained. Or sit in the corner; just know that this party might be the last one you will be invited to for a while. It's up to you.

FIRST ONE IN AND FIRST ONE OUT. If there is a drop-in party you must attend but don't want to stay at, here's our rule: Arrive exactly at start time, and once the fourth guest arrives, leave. If you are the first attendee, your host will always remember that you were present.

NEVER, EVER ARRIVE ten to fifteen minutes early. The final fifteen minutes before the party starts are the most sacred for the busy host, because there are many jobs that cannot be done until the last second: lighting candles, putting out ice, applying lipstick. You don't want to be remembered for having intruded on that holy time.

IF YOU HAVE BEEN INVITED for a quick drink, don't stay longer than 45 minutes to an hour. Any longer is an intrusion, never to be forgotten.

DO NOT HIJACK CONVERSATION. Everybody wants his turn. It's better for people to yearn to hear more from you than to be sick of the sound of your voice.

BE SURE EVERYTHING out of your mouth is positive. If you think someone looks overweight, angry, sad, or tired, don't feel it is necessary to pass this information along. Keep it to yourself. Both Deans have been out on the town and been given unsolicited advice. Our mood instantly plummeted, and we just wanted to go home. Why are some people so tone-deaf?

WHEN YOU ARE INTRODUCED to someone and hit it off with that person, include the introducer the next time you and the new acquaintance get together. You will be honoring that this relationship would not have been formed if not for person A.

"We are curious to see your powder room."

✳ **DO NOT RAMBLE ON TO ONE GUEST** about how beautiful another guest is. One short sentence is plenty, if not too much, on this topic.

✳ **NEVER TOUCH UP YOUR LIPSTICK** at the table at someone's private home, although at a restaurant a quick dab at the table is okay. At your house we are curious to see your powder room anyway (we love them).

※ OH MY GOD, WE HAVE HAD IT! Put down your cell phone! The Deans carry little hammers, smashing cell phones as we go. If your face is pointed down, illuminated by a screen, you better not be anywhere near us.

※ IF YOU BREAK SOMETHING at someone's house and the host is gracious enough to tell you it doesn't matter, do not be fooled. It does matter. Your host is left with one less item than when you arrived. Unacceptable. Always offer to replace it. Craigslist and eBay are great resources for items that are not currently in production. If the item is irreplaceable, you simply cannot go overboard with your apologies after the event, and a handwritten note and some flowers are in order. Never ask if the broken piece was insured. Believe us, we have heard people do this.

※ THANK YOUR HOSTS. A handwritten note trumps all, but e-mail and text are far better than nothing. An old-fashioned phone call is also appreciated, but it must be before lunch the following day.

※ IF YOU GO TO A RESTAURANT, look lively when the check comes. Frequent trips to the bathroom or an absent wallet are not acceptable. The bill does not improve with age, so jump on it early. No need to pay for the entire check but be sure to cover yourself.

A FEW RULES FOR THE HOST:

DO NOT BE THE JUDGE of whether your divorced or divorcing friends can be in the same room together. Invite them both and let them work it out.

YOU MAY HAVE ENVISIONED your party as a coat-and-tie affair, but if any of your guests missed the hint, remove your tie immediately to avoid making him feeling underdressed.

NEVER SEQUESTER YOURSELF where your guests can't see you. They do not know what you are doing, but they know that you are not taking care of them, which causes them to feel rejected. You must be front and center at all times.

TRY TO ORCHESTRATE THE ROOM during cocktails so that people do not speak to their dinner partners. There is nothing in the Deans' universe more disastrous than two people who've exhausted all they have to discuss before the dinner has even started. Hostesses used to post a chart that one could reference upon entering the party, which gave seating for the table. Do the Deans dare suggest reviving this arcane practice?

GETTING YOUR GUESTS TO LEAVE

The Deans have never learned anything after midnight that we ever needed to know. You've given such a successful party that you are faced with a different but still thorny problem. They came, they laughed, they loved, they cried, but they won't go home! What do you do with them?

Stand up, look your guest in the eye, and say, "I know you have a lot to do tomorrow, so I simply cannot take up any more of your time. You've been so generous with it already." They will have to rise to meet you, and then you start walking toward the door.

Another tack could be, "Well, you all have way more energy than I do, and I have to go to bed. You've worn me out." Walk to the front door, open it, and stand next to it until the last guest is on the other side.

Or, when the first person stands up to leave, make a big deal about it, which should prompt everyone else to get a move on. Go stand by the door.

Of course we assume you've already tried the time-tested standbys, such as:

- Blowing out any candles
- Putting away the liquor
- Turning off the music
- Putting on your pajamas

GETTING YOURSELF TO LEAVE

You're at a party and you keep clicking your ruby slippers, but you're not at home yet. What do you do?

The Deans know this feeling well. We've loved the party, but a sense of exhaustion has overcome us. We are in a state of stasis.

Leaving is easier to deal with when you're solo. Getting a still-partying spouse to the door is much more difficult. The single Dean Manigault just stands up, claims a busy tomorrow, and bolts for the door. Like a greasy watermelon, you simply cannot catch her.

The married Dean Pollak, on the other hand, has a verbose spouse who never tires of talking. The Pollaks have never agreed upon a departure signal. Dean Pollak feels that her marriage would be on a surer footing if they had one. We suggest that you and your spouse hurry up and devise a plan. A magical evening can turn into a gripe fest in an instant if one spouse has been dying to leave for hours. Dean Pollak thanks the host, and then stands by her husband until he takes the hint.

Speaking of hints, we are taking one ourselves. This lecture is over.

PART IV

THE DEANS
CONCLUDE

"You are not a slave to Chinese takeout."

We need you to get serious about connecting to your house in a meaningful way. Every home is a living, breathing entity and as such needs love and attention in order to thrive. The quality of everyday living stretched out over a lifetime is far more important than the exclamation marks or grand occasions that punctuate each life haphazardly. We founded the Academy because so many domestic pursuits have ceased to be pursued and therefore people's quality of life is diminishing without their even noticing.

Mopping and ironing are not the sum total of the domestic arts. The arts also include the occasional nap, the family dinner hour, playing cards or monopoly en masse. And the Deans cannot say it enough: Cell phones and computers *must* be left in the other room during the together time. You will never connect with the people around you when you are chained to your PDA. Surely we can put the devices down for an hour or two a day and speak exclusively to the few people with whom we live or have invited over.

When you have learned how to use your house properly, this is what will happen:

YOU ARE GOING TO ENHANCE your bonds with family and friends. When times turn tough, these are the people who will have your back and see you through because they love you and know you so well.

HEALTHFUL LIVING will occur naturally. You are now filling your pantry, freezer, and refrigerator with healthy choices, so when you are hungry and tired you are not a slave to Chinese takeout. You can monitor your portion sizes. After one year don't be surprised if you have lost ten pounds.

YOU WILL HAVE MORE MONEY if you cook at home instead of eating at restaurant, or buying takeout. Eating at a restaurant is the most expensive way to ingest calories.

YOU WILL FIND BALANCE. You must use your house to unwind by drinking a cocktail, reading, doing a crossword, meditating—in short, recharging. Adults benefit from a quiet hour as much as children do.

YOU ARE GOING TO REACH A WIDER CIRCLE by inviting over the people who inspire and interest you. The reason you will do this is because now you have confidence in your cooking and cocktail-making skills, and your kitchen and house are organized. You have practiced having people over with your close friends and now you are ready to expand.

YOUR HOUSE WILL BECOME MORE BEAUTIFUL since you have honed your housekeeping skills. The more time you spend living in your house the more you will come up with ideas on how to improve the quality of your life. It does not take money to feather your nest (and nesting is not the exclusive domain of pregnant women).

A well-functioning house can be a refuge and a launching pad at different points. When a tidal wave hits and knocks you to your knees, if your house is functioning smoothly, it will catch you when you fall. Nothing is more soothing during chaos than a steady routine. At other junctures you are going to yearn for more. You will have mastered your routine and be itching to add a few more elements to it. During these moments you will invite people in to expand your horizons. Your house and you, working as a team, will help woo and entice developments that are as yet unknown to you.

Your house is your biggest financial asset and you must wring the most out of it. At the same time, the four walls eat up your resources every month, so be sure you are extracting all the benefits that a house should provide. Lonely, empty rooms drain a house of energy. Banish all such spaces from your domicile. Make sure every room gets used and laughed in.

Educate your progeny before all these arts are lost. The Deans see lots of money around, but not much lifestyle. Everyone is be-bopping and tweeting away, but they have lost the luxury of a leisured tempo and gracious living. How can your family have stories to pass down if no stories are ever told? And where better to tell these stories than in your own house?

Now that the Deans have gotten everyone and their houses shipshape, it is time for the Deans to pour an Old-Fashioned and put our feet up. It's time for the Deans to rest.

ACKNOWLEDGMENTS

The Deans realize that we had a lot of help along the way. We want to take this opportunity to thank the people who made this book possible.

Emma Sweeney, who got this ball rolling, and our indomitable, lovable, and endlessly supportive agent, Sharon Bowers. Thank you to Leslie Stoker for being the most patient publisher these writers could have ever hoped for. The Deans thank Deb Wood for her meticulous attention to detail and for putting so much thought and work into our book. Sincere thanks to Charles Truax of Truax & Company for his help with the gorgeous illustrations, and the creator of those illustrations, Tania Lee. And to Maris Van Alen, for pointing out when the Deans made too many left turns.

Thanks to Peter Pollak, Pete and Logan Pollak, Caroline and Roger Marandino, Charles Pollak, Christopher Pollak, and Pierre, India, and Gigi Manigault because we earned our PhDs while taking care of all of you. You are fantastic teachers. Now we really must rest!